Praise for *The Sum of Light*

This book meets helpers where they live: in clarity, rigor, and respect for the weight of the work. Grounded in research and operational definitions, it makes a compelling case for self-care not as indulgence, but as professional responsibility. Lara weaves together the empirical and the spiritual from the perspective of experience and with humor and warmth.

What makes the book quietly powerful is that it doesn't remain abstract. Lara offers practical, actionable suggestions for self-care not just for your mind but your body as well. As a martial arts teacher, I found the integration thoughtful and practical. As a counselor, I found it necessary.

With examples and personal insights that offer a genuine glimpse into her world, Lara offers her personal journey to remind us to remember our own. More than offering techniques, this book serves as a compassionate reminder to give ourselves permission to turn our empathy inward—to sharpen the saw rather than grind ourselves down.

Karsten Look, PhD

Adjunct professor of psychology, Columbus College of Art and Design

Sigung in Liu Quan; Sifu of Taoist Kung Fu

If helping others has ever felt overwhelming, too sad, too painful, or too fundamentally unfair, this book is an excellent resource. Funny and accessible, *The Sum of Light* is a roadmap toward caring for yourself as well as for the world you have dedicated yourself to improving.

Lara Palay is a gifted storyteller, entertaining us with witty metaphors that make science and evidence-based healing techniques easy to understand and easy to use. I highly recommend this book.

Susan M. Havercamp, PhD

Professor, Center for Psychiatry and Behavioral Health,

Ohio State University Wexner Medical Center

Recipient of the 2025 Frank J. Menolascino Award for

Excellence in Developmental Disabilities

Drawing on decades of clinical experience and cutting-edge research on empathetic distress, Lara Palay guides helpers through the injuries that can result from caregiving: the vicarious trauma that accumulates silently, the moral injury of systems that ask the impossible, and the slow erosion of the self that comes from giving endlessly.

With remarkable candor, intelligence, humor, and a profound respect for the calling of specialists, she offers practical tools for moving from emotional overwhelm to compassionate presence, reminding readers that tending to ourselves is essential and that our capacity to help others depends on our ability to hold ourselves with the same care.

She skillfully incorporates meditation and other mind-body practices into her work—intelligently venturing into this territory only when she, herself, is familiar with those practices. Palay's highly readable book steps into often-unspoken truths and provides much-needed information and remedies that can benefit caregivers beyond professionals.

Janice Glowski, PhD
Professor, Director of Museum and Galleries at
Otterbein University
Shastri, Columbus Shambhala Center

The Sum of Light

Preventing and Healing Trauma, Moral Injury, and Burnout in the Helping Professions

Lara Palay, LISW-S

This book is dedicated to my sons
Liam and Aidan—
shining bright

Library of Congress Control Number: 2026933645

Copyright ©2026 by the National Association
for the Dually Diagnosed

Published by NADD Press
321 Wall Street, Kingston, N.Y. 12401

ISBN 979-8-9942345-0-1 (paperback)
ISBN 979-8-9942345-1-8 (e-book)

Cover and book design by Mark Sullivan

Chapter Seven
Pausing in the Sacred: Regulation in the Moment | *111*

Chapter Eight
Refilling the Well: Regulation over Time | *125*

Chapter Nine
Angels and Demons: Addiction, Distraction, and Flow | *138*

PART THREE
Reconnecting and Integrating | *159*

Chapter Ten
Doorsteps, Circles, and Baths with Trees: Daily Rituals | *161*

Chapter Eleven
Seven Hours and Three Meals: A Folktale | *174*

Chapter Twelve
Your Body, Electric: Taking Care of Your Instrument | *178*

Chapter Thirteen
The Rhino and the Unicorn: Starting Where You Really Are | *199*

Conclusion
The Sum of Light | *211*

Lara Palay is an expert in therapeutic services for people with intellectual and developmental disabilities. As active members of the NADD organization and collaborators on training projects, I've had the privilege of getting to know her and her work. What has struck me most is the rare combination of depth and practicality that defines her approach. She moves seamlessly from the intricacies of brain science and historical theory to everyday strategies that benefit her readers and colleagues alike.

With *The Sum of Light*, Lara has created a timely and deeply needed book for helping professionals. And who better to offer this perspective than a helping professional herself? She brings years of experience to the table, developing strategies that are both evidence-based and introspective. Her writing merges research and reflection beautifully, offering a guide that is both intellectually rich and emotionally resonant.

This book is filled with examples that make the concepts Lara discusses tangible and applicable to our daily work. Throughout, she connects our need for healing to the shared experience of the COVID-19 pandemic. Her insights are both timely and timeless.

What makes this book truly special is Lara's masterful blending of science and soul. She draws from neuroscience, historical accounts of meditation, and age-old practices, translating them into practical strategies that align with how the brain works. She explains how to stimulate oxytocin, balance cortisol, and tolerate uncomfortable emotions—skills we often teach our clients, but rarely apply to ourselves.

What strikes me most in Lara's writing is her honesty and validation of the inner experience of the practitioner. She openly shares moments when her motivation has flagged or when she's fallen short of being the perfect therapist. Many practitioners feel alone in these struggles, believing they are uniquely failing. Lara's candor gives readers permission to acknowledge these feelings—and shows that doing so is a key step toward managing them and remaining both effective and human.

She offers a clear and compassionate explanation of empathetic distress—feeling the emotional impact of others' trauma—and moral injury, which arises when we act against our values to meet external demands. Lara describes a middle ground: compassionate empathy. This stance allows us to maintain the values that brought us to our work while also preserving our sense of self. In other words, we can hold lofty ideals and still accept the reality that we can't fix everything. And we can still be successful helpers.

Lara also emphasizes the importance of understanding our shadow—the parts of ourselves that don't always live up to our values but are still part of who we are. Drawing from Jungian theory, she describes the shadow as the unconscious, underdeveloped aspects of the self that we often try to suppress. Rather than banishing these parts, Lara encourages us to acknowledge them. Her metaphor of the "wolf in the basement" is a powerful reminder that healing requires us to know and respect all parts of ourselves, even those we find uncomfortable. This is not just psychological insight—it's a call to wholeness.

The final chapters of this book are especially meaningful. Lara gently guides us toward self-forgiveness, helping us release the burden of perfectionism. She reminds us that healing is not about becoming flawless, but about reconnecting with our values, our bodies, and our communities. For me, these chapters offered clarity and comfort—and answered questions I had carried throughout the book. That resolution is best left for Lara to deliver, and I won't spoil it here. But I will say: It's worth the wait.

So, as a reader, I encourage you to take your time with *The Sum of Light*. Much of what Lara offers is meant to be absorbed and experienced, not just learned. Allow yourself to be renewed in a spirit that acknowledges your limitations while affirming that recovery is possible. I am deeply grateful to Lara—and to this book—for reminding me that I, and the people I serve, can be redeemed.

Bruce Davis, PhD

Author of *Fellow Human Beings*

Walking in Jakarta: Helpers, Healers, and Living Dangerously

The Year of Living Dangerously[1] seemed to be in constant rotation on '80s basic cable TV. I was a Gen-Xer with little afterschool supervision, so naturally I watched this movie many times—usually instead of doing my homework. A political thriller set in Indonesia in the 1960s was a strange choice for me to memorize, but as some of you can relate, we latchkey kids were stuck with the same handful of movies—some good, some terrible, many that were pretty adult—that were on TV all the time, chosen with no discernible plan or theme. The result is an odd assortment of films that I can still, 30 years later, quote line for line, and *The Year of Living Dangerously* became one of them. Unlike most of the others (sorry, *Beastmaster*), this movie turned out to mean something for my future.

In one of the early scenes, Guy Hamilton (Mel Gibson) is a naïve Australian journalist experiencing the slums of Jakarta for the first time. Guy walks through streets of desperately poor, starving people who are clawing and pulling at him. His guide through this nightmare underworld is a photographer named Billy Kwan, played by the brilliant Linda Hunt. Billy knows this side of the city and tries to wake up the ambitious, sheltered foreigner. Billy slyly asks an appalled Guy why he doesn't just give one of the beggars the contents of his wallet. "It would be a fortune to him," Billy says. Guy, ever pragmatic, answers that all his cash would not make a dent in their chronic poverty. Billy nods. Tolstoy, Billy says, wrestled with the same problem and despaired, quoting from the gospel of Luke and crying, "What then must we do?"[2] How are we to respond to such overwhelming suffering? What impact can one person make?

As a kid, I certainly missed the more subtle and adult themes of the movie, but this particular scene stayed with me. I came back to it again and again when I grew up and started working with teenagers, some of whom had run away from home to escape violence and exploitation. As a young social worker, fully as naïve as Guy, I had a vague notion that if I worked hard enough, and pushed others to work hard, I could somehow have a mathematical impact—reducing the total number of problems in the world. As I got older, I began to understand the scope of what I was actually doing. I realized that while social change was certainly possible, the reality was that I, myself, was unlikely to accomplish much—not if you looked at all of the suffering in all of the world. There would always be parents who abused or neglected their children. Those children would grow to be angry, sad teens who would struggle, cause violence and harm to others (maybe), and then have babies themselves. Then *their* babies would grow up, and on and on. The pain and sadness that human beings were capable of carrying within themselves, and then passing on to others, seemed bottomless, limitless. It was hard not to feel despair. What then must I do?

As I learned about trauma and it became the wellspring of my work and my thinking, I was inevitably drawn back to this question. Now I had lived long enough to see the wear and tear, the road damage trauma work had inflicted on me as well, listening to story after story, sometimes stepping into nightmares as I visited clients and families in homes filled with chaos, anger, and depression. I had experienced the isolation and fatigue of not telling the people closest to me about the things I had seen. It was important to me to protect my family from some of the horror I knew was in the world, and I was glad to do it, but it could be a lonely feeling to come home some days to the question "How was work?" and answer "Fine." Burnout became a very real threat looming in my professional life, and I lectured and wrote about burnout and its components. I started learning more about the emerging science of "compassion fatigue" (more correctly named "empathetic distress," but we'll get to that). I started to feel some mastery of the topic.

And then the pandemic came.[3]

I saw that I was my own living experiment, observing the effects of constant stress and fear as I tried to help other people in the same situation I was in. As I've written about elsewhere, helping someone in emotional distress means tolerating their emotions, recognizing and acknowledging them without letting yourself be overwhelmed by them. We refer to this in a lot of ways; "holding space" is a popular term these days. I've always thought of it as "containing." My odd, associative brain always sees that emotional container I bring to my clients as a woven basket for apples, maybe because apples are wholesome and each one contains the seeds of something new at its heart. I hold out this imaginary basket between us, and the client puts their apples into it   the memories, emotions, thoughts, and beliefs they've carried, usually alone, sometimes for a very long time. And then I hold that basket full of apples for as long as they need me to, until they slowly take the apples back, one by one, to look over and choose. The rotten ones can be tossed. The whole and healthy apples can be kept. My clients rearrange the apples they decide to keep, and the pile that was once overspilling and burdensome is now sorted. They can tell their story with a more compassionate, more true arrangement of the facts of their lives. They begin to grow, and they nurture the understanding and self-acceptance they want to carry forward.

It occurs to me that this image may be a telling one. The basket is something *I hold in my hands*, not a space inside myself. I think an intuitive part of my psyche knew early on that a seemingly small distinction like this might turn out to be important, saving me from the direct impact of absorbing the distressing stories and the heartbreak each apple represents. Still, that basket gets heavy sometimes. Then, starting in the spring of 2020, I was suddenly holding many more apples, while needing a place for *my* apples as well. It all became too much for me, as it did for you and any other helpers during this time. And it wasn't just clients. I was trying to help the people I loved, too. My friends and family were used to being able to call or text me when they were scared or sad, and I would be available to help, or at least listen, and that was usually OK. Now it had become—to carry this metaphor to its inevitable and ridiculous conclusion—an avalanche of apples. Some days I felt the weight of every single one of them—and worse, I felt the weight of my guilt at my failure to carry them. After all, wasn't I an apple expert? How was it that I was failing so spectacularly at practicing what I preached? The burden of the helper suddenly seemed like something I might not be able to handle after all. And if I was not a helper, what was I?

I need to say here that I am well aware that my pandemic was very, very easy compared to the pandemics of other people—maybe including you. I didn't have school-aged children at home, my parents were able to isolate and stay safe relatively easily, and I was able to shift immediately to completely remote work. Contrast that with the hospital worker, the home-based, shift-working staff, the caregivers with family members at risk or in the hospital or dying, cut off from family and comfort, while that staff person had to keep working to provide for them. Yep, my pandemic was a day at the park when placed up against all that. Nevertheless, it was a high tide for me, and I was drowning. I startled myself when I burst into tears in my doctor's office, saying that I couldn't sleep and that I might not be OK (knowing guiltily that she probably wasn't OK, either). Normally, I'd have tried to be professional, cool, and funny while hinting at this little problem I might have. Not this time. I just couldn't keep it together anymore. I found that all the things I thought I knew deeply and intimately were just the beginning of my *real* understanding of the dangers to us helpers, the carriers of the baskets, the holders of space for nightmares. We must equip ourselves to continue doing what we love and what we need to do in the face of some of these dangers. That is why you are holding this book now.

I also wanted to write this because I seem to need constant reminders not to minimize my feelings, even in the face of the much worse suffering of others. It seems that I am not alone in this, because I hear other helpers do the same thing all the time, with black humor or shrugs of dismissal. "It's not a big deal," "It's what I see all the time," "You should hear some of the stories I listen to, and you wouldn't be so worried about this little thing," and so on. When I read Gabor Maté's most recent book, *The Myth of Normal*,[4] two statements early in the book jumped out at me.

The first comes on page 20 of the hardcover edition: "Trauma is not what happens to you but what happens *inside* you" [italics in original].[5] This wasn't a new idea to me, but Maté had stated a familiar truth in an unfamiliarly simple and elegant way. Yes, my pandemic was easier than many other people's. Yes, what you go through at work isn't as devastating as a single life-destroying event one of your clients may have suffered. Yes, yes, yes. There is truth in that perspective. But it is also true that trauma is what goes on inside of you. It cannot be measured by rulers ("this trauma is easier; that trauma is worse") outside of you and your own experience. I assume that all of us come to this book carrying some amount of hurt.

The next thing that struck me was even more on the nose. Maté quotes his colleague, the great trauma therapist and writer Peter Levine, who says, "Trauma is perhaps the most avoided, ignored, belittled, denied, misunderstood, and untreated cause of human suffering."[6] We are used to reading that sentence and thinking immediately about the clients we serve, the oppressed groups for whom we fight, or the latest soul-destroying story we saw on the news. We think of others. I invite you to go back now and read it again, and this time, *think only about yourself.*

How did that feel? My guess is that if you picked up this book and read this far, that sentence hits a target somewhere inside you.

When I started writing this book, I thought and (surprise!) worried about how I could possibly communicate everything we know about empathetic distress, burnout, and the harm that can come from seeing to and doing too much for others and not seeing to and doing for ourselves. How could I summarize every book, every article, with more coming out every day? The answer, of course, is that I couldn't. But finally, I reached a decision: Maybe I couldn't write about all of it, but that was OK, because I didn't really want to do that anyway. I *did* want to write a book that did two things.

First, I wanted to talk about things I care about, the things I have learned about how to do this sort of work and keep doing it, despite all that we see and hear that many people will never know or understand. How we keep ourselves from getting too tired, too angry, and too soul-sick to keep going.

Second, I wanted a book that would be useful; to distill some of the pool of information that grows wider and deeper every day, and then hand you a little bottle of it to put in your pocket. This bottle wouldn't have a magical potion in it, unfortunately, but maybe it could be medicine you could carry with you and use when you needed it.

In this book, I talk about therapists, doctors, nurses, social workers, soldiers, direct service professionals, mental health paraprofessionals, executives, first responders, other people who work in mental health, other people who work in intellectual and developmental disability (IDD) and dual diagnosis, brain cells, unicorns, the Trojan War, and Mister Rogers. Some examples will be closer to your experience than others, of course, but still, with such a wide range, you might be wondering: Who on earth is this book for?

This book is for you:

A frontline worker, paraprofessional, or DSP.

A clinician.

A supervisor.

A first responder.

A social worker.

A teacher.

A nurse.

A doctor.

A leader.

. . . wherever you are on the helper's path.

How to Use This Book

I've talked a little about a lot of things in this book, so much so that whatever resonates for you here will almost certainly not be all you need to know about that thing. I have included a list of my major sources and a list of recommended reading to help you go deeper, but hopefully this book will help you get started.

We'll explore the special kinds of trauma we helpers are vulnerable to, and how to tell the difference between good old garden-variety stress and traumatizing levels of overwhelm and pain. I describe a little of the still largely mysterious terrain of moral injury, that crippling guilt and grief that can come to helpers when they cannot do what they have dedicated themselves to doing or when they have simply seen too much. Next, I talk about the nature of emotions, which are, after all, the raw material for stress, both good and bad. We'll look briefly together at how we understand problems of living—and how we might shift our understanding to a more realistic view.

We take a turn then, because it's important to me that you find something you can use the minute you set this book down. I explore our emerging understanding of what I believe "compassion fatigue" really is—empathetic distress—and how we helpers can use this new science in a practical way to position ourselves in a stance of protective, compassionate empathy when we're working. I look at the difference between Distraction and Flow. We'll talk about how to listen to the deep signals from ourselves. I bring in some of the oldest wisdom humans have access to and talk about rituals, the small (or big) practices that can help us move from one world to another and remind us, at the most profound level, that we are more than our workplace, our emails, our responsibilities, and our worries.

Next comes a quick update on how we are understanding the brain-body connection—not really a connection at all, but one united field of being, notionally broken into components but best understood as one shimmering whole. Finally, I bring all this together and look at how we can hold our own baskets of apples, maintaining a compassionate, open heart toward ourselves as well as the world we've dedicated ourselves to improving. As with my previous book, there is space at the end for you to reflect and make notes if you like.

A ROADMAP FOR HEALING OURSELVES:
HERMAN'S TASKS OF HEALING

One way to think about this book is as a roadmap for healing ourselves, much the way therapists lay out roadmaps for clients healing from trauma or grief. In my first book, I mentioned the foundational work on trauma by Judith Herman, as expressed in her book *Trauma and Recovery.*[7] When I taught trauma, I used her overview of trauma therapy. This does not mean that every technique she writes about is one that I use; there's room for a lot of variation based on the individual client and therapist sitting together in a consulting room. Still, over the years, I've found that her understanding of healing is universal, despite the wide variety of approaches that might come under that framework. She writes that there are three stages, or what I prefer, *tasks* of trauma work: Safety and Stabilization, Mourning and Remembrance, and Reconnection and Integration. I've used these three tasks to frame this book. In parts one, two, and three, I include themes you can consider and reflect on, particularly in how ideas of safety, mourning, or reconnection might take shape for you.

Safety and Stabilization
Many clients come to trauma therapy in very activated states, and they may be doing things to soothe or numb themselves that are harmful or even life-threatening, like self-harm, hard drugs, or placing themselves

in dangerous situations. Many are actively thinking about killing themselves; some have already tried. Obviously, the first order of business is to establish some safe ground, whether that means helping them to escape an actively threatening environment or learning how to be safe with themselves. Crisis plans, emergency resources, and building a trusting relationship in therapy occupy most of the work in therapy at this point. You might be noticing ways you want to build safety at your workplace, in your network of support, or in your personal relationships. We'll talk about signals in your body, sensations, feelings, and thoughts that may mean you're getting overwhelmed or triggered. You'll have a chance to learn how to feel strong feelings with some new skills for observing and supporting them, without clinging to or avoiding them. I will argue that even a conversation about how we take care of ourselves is a form of creating our own Safety and Stabilization.

Mourning and Remembrance

This is about going through what happened, if that's useful, and more importantly, it's learning to experience and release what happens in the brain and body when we've held fear and pain for too long. You may have painful memories that come up, or you may have to grieve things that should have happened but didn't. This might apply directly to you, but, of course, since this is a book about the vicarious effects of the suffering of others, you might be grieving for your clients or coworkers. You might mourn some parts of yourself that feel damaged or lost to you. This is normal and OK. There are literally hundreds of books on this part of trauma work, and much of that is outside our scope here, but I do draw from that theme. We will also identify what we experience in the moment and how to work with it. I think that identifying the meaning in our work is an element of remembrance and can help heal distress from our exposure to suffering, so it is included in this section as well.

Reconnection and Integration

After finding stable ground and recognizing our emotions, I usually work with clients on the long process of reconnecting to things that have been severed or lost. To talk about this, I'll use the three layers of trauma Bessel van der Kolk talks about in *The Body Keeps the Score*. Briefly, he talks about the essential damage trauma does to our sense of self—emotionally, cognitively, and physically. I talk about this in more detail in my book, *The Way Through*, and you'll see this language many times throughout this book. Regulating, grounding, or getting into your body are different ways of talking about integration. Integration here just means that all the parts are working together, communicating, and no one part is running away with all the other ones. In trauma therapy, integration can mean, "I've looked at what happened, worked on it, and now it's a part of my life, but it isn't my whole life. It's a part of me, but it's not all of me." Learning how to stay in our bodies, feeling, processing, and thinking in something like real time is a long process. The next level might be called healing the wound in relationships. This could be relationships in our close circle, or with a partner, but it means being able to relate to some Other without consistent masking, dissociating, or shutting down. Finally, trauma survivors have to find a way to connect with the society around them. For soldiers, this might mean giving back to their community rather than thinking their experiences have made them unfit to be around other people. For some trauma survivors, helping other people to heal or working in groups to collaborate on creative projects can be a life-affirming way to connect with society.

Reconnection may be something literal, such as finding supportive people in your world or connecting to spirit, nature, or culture. *Integration* can also be the culmination of all the ideas in the book: integrating what has hurt and needed to be seen and healed with what is most important to us as helpers into the larger, balanced selves we need to be.

These themes are just one way to read the book, so if they speak to you, great; if not, leave them, and that's good too.

UNDER THE AWESOME

I once had a client describe an over-functioning, always-giving family member who, in her opinion, needed to "get under the awesome." She meant that this person needed to stop trying to build a shield of everything-is-great-and-look-how-well-I'm-doing and deal with their pain, rather than achieving it all and doing it all to avoid feeling.

I think that a lot of you reading this book (and certainly the person writing it) can be described this same way sometimes. We *can* do it all: work a crazy job, help every friend, keep our families' lives running smoothly, and never complain or get fed up. If you are someone who over-copes, I discuss this in depth later in this book. But even just reading this introduction might feel scary or a little threatening to consider going "under the awesome" in your own life. It's like the soldier who can't afford to set her heavy pack down and take off her boots, because if she does, she'll never get them back on, and she won't have the strength to pick up all her weapons and all her survival tools and start marching again. If you're a little afraid of this, keep reading. We'll unpack it all, and I hope it will help. Things will feel lighter. You won't worry about stopping, taking breaks, or making changes in your life to fit you better.

But if you are *very afraid* of doing this, and the thought of looking deeply at your life makes you feel panicky or numb, put this book down right now. Find a compassionate family member, friend, or colleague who can support you while you get a doctor or therapist to work with you. Your life *can* change, you *can* feel healthy and comfortable living it, and *you deserve that.* We all deserve lives in which we feel safe and OK—it's our God-given, inalienable right as human beings. But you need help and support so that it doesn't feel overwhelming. I'd rather have you read my book later, or not at all, than for you to feel so distressed that you don't take any steps and stay frozen and scared. Take your time, get the understanding and aid you are entitled to, and start from there.

We do live dangerously in these professions we've chosen. Burnout, trauma, and overexposure to distress can do real damage to us, and some of it may be hard to heal. Those of us who work with the extremely vulnerable, such as people with dual diagnoses, physical disabilities, severe persistent mental illnesses, and the like, may also grapple with the added pressure to help when society seems to only want to ignore. I've included some statistics and data here and there, and you can find my sources at the end, along with some recommended reading if you want to go further into some of the topics. But this is not meant to be an academic book or a complete picture of the vast (and widening) crisis of emotional distress in helping professionals. While I share the major concepts and emerging research I think are useful, I chose to write mostly from my experience and what I have learned from this subject. My hope for you reading this book is that you'll find something useful in it. If that makes you a better staff person, a better manager or executive, a better therapist or crisis worker, that's good news for your little part of the world, and I'm glad to have played a role in bringing that about. But if all this book does is make you a little better at *caring for and valuing yourself*, that's enough. You are also deserving of care; you are also a part of the world you're here to help, and I am grateful you are in it. Our ability to care and connect might be the most important thing we have to offer, and the most essential thing we need to receive.

> The feelings which we think of as "positive" and "constructive" are a reaching-out, an effort to make contact and establish some sort of communication. Feelings of love and kindness, the ability to care and empathize ... are efforts to link and integrate; they are the emotions that bring us together, if not in fact then at least in a comforting illusion that makes the burden of mortality a little easier to bear ...
>
> [T]hey are all we know of the light.
>
> —Stephen King, *Danse Macabre*[8]

CHAPTER ONE

Blast Radius and Haunted Houses: Secondary Traumatic Stress and Vicarious Trauma

"How could the world go back to the way it was when so much bad has happened?"

—J.R.R. Tolkien, *The Lord of the Rings*

When we talk about the effects of a trauma that we haven't personally experienced, we're going to call it *secondary traumatic stress* or *vicarious trauma*.[9] There is some confusion on which term means what, and experts differ in how they apply them. Here's how I distinguish them: For me, *secondary* implies gradations or maybe degrees of exposure from a given event. An example could be "ground zero," perhaps the factory where an explosion took place. If you were at ground zero at the factory, inside the building, or outside near the loading dock doors, you were directly hit. Let's say that the next ring out from that factory site is a mile wide: If you were in that second zone, maybe you could hear the explosion, or you felt your windows rattle, but you weren't affected in the same way as someone in the direct path of the flying metal and shards of glass. It makes sense to me that this second range of a traumatic event would include the people immediately on the scene after an event (firefighters arriving moments after the explosion) or directly involved with helping (a physician or nurse in the ER treating a victim of the accident). Sometimes I also see the term *critical incident stress* to describe this kind of reaction, and that works too. To keep things simple, I'm going to stick with secondary traumatic stress and vicarious trauma, but some of the sources listed at the end of the book may use others. The American Counseling Association suggests that vicarious trauma, compassion fatigue, secondary traumatic stress, and secondary victimization can all be considered roughly synonymous, and they place them all under the sad, simple umbrella: "the cost of caring."[10]

When we use the word *vicarious*, it typically refers to something happening *through* something else, such as "I vicariously relived my high school drama-nerd days when my son was cast in the school play."[11] In the same way, I might vicariously feel fear or helplessness when someone is telling me about a trauma that happened to them thirty years ago—my experience of it is solely through them and their telling of it. So, I use *secondary traumatic stress* to refer to the distress that we may experience on the scene, or immediately dealing with the results, of a trauma that did not affect us directly. I use *vicarious trauma* to refer to being exposed only through the story, feelings, or behaviors resulting from a trauma someone else experienced, possibly years and miles away from us.

BLAST RADIUS: SECONDARY TRAUMATIC STRESS

An EMT wasn't there when someone took the fentanyl and overdosed, but she is the first one to treat the unconscious body. A nurse deals with the burn wounds from an accident that happened minutes earlier, though he himself is not hurt. A victim advocate talks to the rape survivor while their clothes still bear the evidence of the crime. Some helping professionals are exposed to this kind of trauma every day, and while that has its own challenges, there is a sort of preparedness they develop, like putting on a suit of mental armor before heading into work (though as we'll see, that has its limits).

Where I think this stress can be sneakier and thus harder to recognize and support is when it occurs only occasionally. The disability field is a good example. My business partner and I were once conducting a series of daylong training sessions for a large provider of IDD services, including day programs and group homes. Each audience we spoke to that week had about a hundred people from across the agency. Among them were direct service workers, and we offered multiple training sessions so that people who worked shifts had a good chance to attend one. That day, we were scheduled to begin at 8 in the morning, and we knew several of the homes would have staff joining us directly after their overnight shifts ended. This is a familiar challenge for us—we have to be lively and engaging enough to keep tired staff awake. But this time was different.

Just before we went on stage, an agency executive came up to us, looking shaken. He told us that one of the residents in a group home had a severe choking episode early that morning and nearly died on the scene. Fortunately, EMTs were able to revive her, and she was recovering in the hospital. The problem now was that the staff, who had all been involved in this, were coming directly from work to our training, with no time to decompress or process their feelings. Sure enough, just as the supervisor was telling us this, we turned and saw four or five staff members slowly walking into the large conference center. They looked pale and slightly dazed, heading straight for their chairs and sitting frozen and silent, not milling around, grabbing breakfast pastries, or socializing the way the others were. After a quick huddle, we shifted the morning events. After a brief introduction, we started right into several breathing and grounding exercises rather than doing them later in the day as we'd planned. With one eye on those staff, we went through the morning, and I could see them gradually relax and start to attend to what was going on around them.

These staff members did exactly what they were supposed to do in that emergency. When they tried the first aid steps to clear the resident's obstructed airway, it didn't work. They called 911, the woman in their care was treated, and she lived. Everyone did everything right in this story. There was no lack of training or support to point to; it was just something that occasionally happens and is beyond anyone's control. But I could see on their faces how shocking, upsetting, and disorienting this was for them. They weren't the ones who nearly died, but they carried some traces of traumatic stress from simply being present for it.

Risk Factors for Secondary Traumatic Stress

Anyone who deals with human suffering and aggression is at risk for exposure to this kind of traumatic stress. Of course, just like with trauma, as I talked about in *The Way Through*, not everyone who is exposed to this stress will develop ongoing problems with it. Professions that are particularly vulnerable include law enforcement, medical professionals (especially in emergency care), child welfare, first responders, and social workers who deal with crisis, educators, administrators, and others. Really, any profession in which we experience the suffering of other beings, including animals, should be included on that list.

There are many ways of categorizing the symptoms of secondary and vicarious traumatic stress. The ones I find most helpful feature the things we may notice in our bodies, in our thoughts, in our feelings, in our behavior (especially at work), and in our interactions with others. Some lists will have items I have not included here, but I think this gives you an idea of how this stress manifests itself in us.

Somatic/Body

- Exhaustion
- Nausea/vomiting
- Weakness
- Difficulty breathing
- Chest pains
- Rapid heart rate
- Headaches
- Dry mouth/always thirsty
- Elevated blood pressure
- Fainting/dizziness
- Worsening allergy problems
- Symptoms of shock
- Onset or worsening of chronic pain or autoimmune issues[12]

Emotional

- Frustration
- Strong need for recognition of what they experienced
- Anxiety
- Guilt/strong feelings for victims
- Sense of loss
- Anger
- Denial
- Fear of loss of control
- Irritability/agitation
- Depression
- Feelings of overwhelm
- Feelings of isolation
- Loss of emotional control

Cognitive/Thinking

- Blaming attitude
- Confusion
- Reduced attention span
- Flashbacks
- Poor concentration
- Negative self-talk/loss of confidence
- Decreased awareness
- Troubled thoughts
- Nightmares
- Distraction
- Short-term memory disturbance
- Time/place/person distortion

Behavior

- Emotional outbursts
- Changes in activity level
- Disturbed sleep
- Increase in smoking
- Easily startled/hypervigilance
- Antisocial behavior
- Withdrawal
- Changes in eating habits (increase or decrease in food consumption)
- Difficulty relaxing
- Fidgety/restless
- Increased use of alcohol and other drugs
- Changes in sex drive

In any of the helping professions, secondary traumatic stress is like a bomb waiting to go off. How prepared we are for the explosion, how close we are, and how often we get hit with the shrapnel may determine how we do for a while, but given enough explosions, any level of exposure starts to take a toll.

How widespread is this problem? There are a lot of people getting caught in the blasts. It's hard to talk about with any precision, but here are some statistics to give you an idea:

For nurses, exhaustion scores on the Maslach Burnout Inventory were 16, and for direct care/supervisory staff, 37. A score of 30 is the cutoff for indicating burnout.[13]

Among health care aides, direct care staff, and support workers, depersonalization (which can be a symptom of trauma and an indicator of burnout) was high, at 34%.[14]

Doctors in the US report more exhaustion than in Canada and the Netherlands, in a study conducted before the pandemic.[15]

People who work in healthcare professions and face heavy workloads, long shifts, high consequences for errors, depression, anxiety, PTSD, emotional exhaustion, professional isolation, challenging interpersonal and occupational dynamics, and ready access to lethal means are at an increased risk of suicide.[16]

If secondary traumatic stress is a bomb, then vicarious trauma is a ghost.

HAUNTED HOUSES: VICARIOUS TRAUMA

"Folk wisdom is filled with ghosts who refuse to rest in their graves until their stories are told."

—Judith Herman, *Trauma and Recovery*

When I was six, my parents took my little sister and me to Disney World. I don't remember much of that trip, but I have a vivid picture in my head of the Haunted Mansion ride. We were wheeled in little cars on tracks through darkened rooms, each with scary stage settings of a decaying house. Moans and shrieks played on the loudspeakers. At one point, the cars twirled us around a corner to a face a mirrored wall, and in that instant, I could see a ghostly green skeleton, magically lounging in the car. It was sitting right beside me! Shocked, I whipped my head around to look at it, and of course, it wasn't there. A camera mounted on the wall behind us had projected the image onto the mirror in front of us. I looked again and again, from the ghost I could see in the mirror to the empty seat next to me, trying to understand. Later, my parents explained to me how it was done.

Being around someone who is reacting to something you can't see can feel like many things, but one word that always comes to my mind is *eerie*. It's disorienting, like that ride. For example, I've been in the middle of an argument with a shelter resident about how long they could use the house phone (this was before cell phones). Battered, with a long, twisting cord, the wall-mounted phone in the common area of our shelter was always in high demand. There was a sign-up sheet and a time limit for calls. The dispute with my adolescent client would start at a normal pitch. The two teams: Annoyed and Demanding (the resident) and Annoyed and Overworked (me). We would argue. Then, with no warning, it would seem as though we had launched to another plane of reality. Suddenly, the resident was screaming and ranting, accusing me of doing things I didn't recognize or that clearly had nothing to do with our situation. Occasionally, they would have an oddly blank expression in their eyes while this was happening. With experience, I understood that they were no longer upset about the phone or even at me. They might not even be seeing me anymore. They were reacting to something (or someone) from before, maybe long before the two of us came to be standing by that phone. It was as if one of the ghosts from the Haunted Mansion had joined us, and I couldn't see it—but they could.

What I've learned in the years since is that in most of those situations, the resident was triggered into some past trauma. If they were not having an actual flashback to a specific incident, then they were at least locking into fighting as if using that grubby phone was a matter of life and death. Sometimes I could almost feel the real battles they must have fought or witnessed in the past, presumably over matters far mor important than making a call. It was disconcerting and weird when this happened—especially if the person had that flat look, like they'd taken a little "mental vacation" while they were screaming at me.

As I mentioned in *The Way Through*, there are many neurological conditions that our clients or individuals with IDD might have. Some disorders, especially those that cause focal emotional seizures,[17] can make someone look momentarily blank and then behave oddly, maybe lashing out in rage. But for most of us, most of the time, we are more likely to be dealing with an emotional outburst than a neurological anomaly.

This is one of the most insidious traps for people working in the IDD field. As a trauma therapist, I often see clients who have come specifically for trauma therapy. Even if that's not the case, I'm mentally prepared that the intense emotions or upsetting story of a trauma may be part of our session. I can take a deep breath, ground myself, and mentally prepare for that intensity. But you can't do that if you don't know that's what you're dealing with.

Let's say you're making a spaghetti dinner with one of the individuals you support. You start talking about Sunday dinners from childhood or how your grandmother taught you her special recipe for sauce. Your individual responds to this by saying, "One time, my daddy punched my mom because he said he didn't want s'ketti. We were crying and saying to him to *stop*, but he didn't stop. Blood got everywhere, and she went in the ambulance. That's when I went to live with my grandma." That was a trauma narrative, and you had no warning. You didn't see it coming.

It's jolting and upsetting to be hit with such a painful story when you aren't expecting it, but that's not even the hardest situation. Even more stressful—and eerie—might be when you are in the presence of someone reacting out of fear or rage, but they cannot tell you anything about it. People with limited or no speech, and possibly no awareness of what is happening inside them can't really let you know what is wrong. There are few things scarier or more heartbreaking to me than watching the terror and horror of someone's trauma being acted out in front of me, with absolutely no explanation or context. There's no moment to take a breath and prepare, the way I do before I walk into my consulting room to start a session. There aren't clear indications of what is about to happen.

When you work in a field that is not expressly dedicated to it, trauma sneaks up on you, surprises you, and you don't have the armor you need in place to understand or cope with it. This is vicarious trauma. You weren't there at all. You might glimpse the story—like hearing about the disastrous spaghetti dinner—or you may only feel it, like a ghost you can't see but whose presence sends a chill through the room. You may feel this down the years and hundreds of miles away, without a way to pin down what set everything in motion.

"Secondary traumatic stress [also "vicarious trauma"] is the emotional duress that results when an individual hears about the first-hand trauma experiences of another."[18] In contrast, vicarious trauma is "the negative transformation in the helper that results (across time) from empathic engagement with trauma survivors and their traumatic material, combined with a commitment or responsibility to help them. For therapists, welfare workers, case managers, and other helping professionals involved in the care of traumatized people, the essential act of listening to trauma stories may take an emotional toll that compromises professional functioning and diminishes quality of life."[19]

I want to highlight *time:* We know that these effects usually do not show up after one bad day or one tough client. It can be more like a drop of water wearing away at a stone, and it's helpful to remind yourself that if you've been doing this work for a while, you may have started to experience these effects even if you don't have some dramatic event you can point to in your work history. Simply working the field puts you at risk.[20]

I've compiled the most common symptoms I've found for vicarious trauma, and you'll see how much they overlap with secondary traumatic stress.

VICARIOUS TRAUMA SYMPTOMS

- Difficulty managing emotions
- Feeling emotionally numb or shut down
- Fatigue, sleepiness, or difficulty falling asleep
- Physical problems or complaints, such as aches, pains, and decreased resistance to illness
- Being easily distracted, which can increase one's risk of accidents
- Loss of a sense of meaning in life and/or feeling hopeless about the future
- Relationship problems (e.g., withdrawing from friends and family, increased interpersonal conflicts, avoiding intimacy)

- Feeling vulnerable or worrying excessively about potential dangers in the world and loved ones' safety
- Increased irritability; aggressive, explosive, or violent outbursts and behavior
- Destructive coping or addictive behaviors (e.g., over/undereating, substance abuse, gambling, taking undue risks in sports or driving)
- Lack of or decreased participation in activities that used to be enjoyable
- Avoiding work and interactions with clients or constituents
- A combination of symptoms that comprise a diagnosis of Posttraumatic Stress Disorder (PTSD)

Trauma therapists J. Eric Gentry and Jeffrey Dietz compared the Diagnostic and Statistical Manual (DSM) symptoms of PTSD with symptoms of secondary or vicarious trauma and created a list that combines the two.[21] While some of the symptoms related to caregivers overlap with those we've already seen in this chapter, many have been adapted specifically to the helping professions. They do list hypervigilance, but I find the language in that category so similar to the DSM language that I did not include it here.

For the intrusive symptoms of PTSD, they suggest the following:
- Having frequent dreams or nightmares about work
- Becoming preoccupied with particular patients or clients
- Letting patient/work issues encroach on your personal time
- Seeing yourself as a "savior," the only one who knows how to properly care for others
- Feeling a sense of entitlement that causes you to flout rules or ignore conventions

- Constantly thinking and feeling inadequate about your role as a care provider
- Categorizing everyone as either a potential victim or a potential perpetrator, perceiving the world as increasingly dangerous[22]

For avoidance:
- Tuning out clients when they tell you about their traumatic experiences
- Losing interest in activities you once enjoyed or abandoning self-care activities
- Pervasive feelings of fatigue or hopelessness
- Dreading routine tasks or the prospect of working with particular patients
- Losing confidence in your competence/effectiveness as a caregiver
- Withdrawing from friends and family to spend long hours engaging in escapist pursuits such as watching television or online gaming
- Using alcohol, drugs, sex, food shopping, or other self-soothing strategies to ward off feelings of fear, anxiety, or depression
- Increased conflicts with loved ones who express worries about your behavior

For negative alterations in cognition and mood:
- Feelings of detachment or estrangement from colleagues and patients
- Feeling cynical or hopeless about your caregiving career
- Inability to draw pleasure or satisfaction from caregiving successes and inordinate concern with perceived caregiving failures

- Distorted perception of yourself as either inadequate or superior
- Blaming patients and colleagues for poor outcomes
- Difficulty summoning the energy needed to fulfill caregiving responsibilities
- Abandoning relationships or interests that once sustained you

I'd add that some of the less familiar manifestations of trauma might apply here as well, including hoarding, disorganization, and clutter. The potential link between these experiences and trauma is still being investigated by researchers.[23]

How Can You Tell If You Might Have Secondary or Vicarious Traumatic Stress?

First things first: This is not a book I want you to use to diagnose yourself with *anything*. As Peter Levine says, "[A]ll traumatic events are stressful, but not all stressful events are traumatic,"[24] and in Chapter Twelve, we'll talk about the good kinds of stress and go into more depth about allostatic load and how we all, as organisms, deal with and even *need* some kinds of stress.

For now, I found this set of statements about normal stress really helpful. I've simplified the language a bit, and at the end of the book, they appear again in a questionnaire format so you can spend more time with them. Maté simply points out that you can start to see a shift when stress goes from manageable to more than we can handle—and that's when we may be talking about trauma. Here are some examples of what he describes as stress that is manageable and not traumatizing:

"It is not trauma if the following remain true over the long term:

It does not limit you, constrict you, diminish your capacity to think or feel or trust or assert yourself, to experience suffering without succumbing to despair or to witness it with compassion.

It does not keep you from holding your pain and sorrow and fear without being overwhelmed and without having to escape habitually into work or compulsive self-soothing or self-stimulating by whatever means.

You are not left compelled either to aggrandize yourself or to efface yourself for the sake of gaining acceptance or to justify your existence.

It does not impair your capacity to experience gratitude for the beauty and wonder of life"[25]

As you go through this list, pay attention to your body, your feelings, and your thoughts. Does anything on this list register on one or more of those three levels? Don't jump to any conclusions, but take the time to sit with this. There is space at the end of the book to write your answers or take notes, and that might be a helpful way to let your reaction point you toward your next steps. You might decide to take action, make changes, or just tune in more and learn what might be going on for you. No matter what, take your time with this.

Whether it's explosions or phantoms, we who work with these kinds of injuries deserve our own patience, attention, and time—just the same as what we offer our clients. Be as good to yourself as you are to them, and don't rush to judgment.

CHAPTER TWO

Lost to Ourselves: Moral Injury

IN MEMORY OF

THE ELDERLY WOMAN

I KILLED IN VIETNAM

FORGIVE ME. I'M SO SORRY

GENE SIMMERS

—cenotaph for an unknown victim of war, Gene Simmers, veteran[26]

Moral injury is a term I used to bring up in my classes about trauma and grief. At the time, it was not heard much outside of combat PTSD, but in fact, soldiers have been talking about moral injury, in one way or another, as far back as the ancient Greeks. In my brief dips into conversations in the medical community, I heard the term occasionally, as nurses and doctors talked about the creeping damage they were seeing in themselves and their colleagues, simply from the constant strain of our current medical system. Then the pandemic hit, and the phrase *moral injury* is now heard everywhere. When I talk about this to audiences, I usually start by explaining it this way:

With PTSD, we're usually talking about *something that was done to us* or something we witnessed. Moral injury is usually caused by *something we did to someone else,* or failed to do for them.

In most of our likely experiences of it, moral injury is what happens when, by our actions or failure to act, we can no longer see ourselves the way we once did. In some cases, seeing the immense pain one human can inflict on another may damage our ability to see *anyone* as truly good or moral. Maybe we can't see ourselves as a good person anymore. In its extreme form (again, usually in combat conditions or something extraordinarily horrifying), we may no longer even feel human.

Clinicians are familiar with this in some cases of trauma, where the survivor of the trauma was also required to inflict damage on someone else, either under duress or confusion. Cult members report struggling with moral injury if they helped to entice or keep someone in the cult. Severe moral injury can be unbelievably damaging, and it takes time and skilled help to heal.

As usual, this may sound far away from your day in the helping professions, and it's true that you may never be exposed to its most virulent forms. But if we break down the definition and causes of moral injury, it might start to sound less foreign to you.

Moral injury in helpers can be caused by:

- being exposed to upsetting images/situations of harm to others
- doing things that violate your view of yourself as a good or helpful person
- feeling let down by the systems that lead or support you

The beginning stage, or milder form of moral injury, is *moral distress,* just as traumatic stress can lead to a more formal classification of a full-blown disorder.

Moral distress has two subtypes: constraint distress and uncertainty distress.[27]

CONSTRAINT DISTRESS

Constraint distress is what helpers experience when they cannot help or rescue someone they feel a desire to help. The doctor who has to turn patients away from an overrun hospital, the EMT who can't save the overdosing teenager, the home-based worker who cannot visit her families in person, all share some part of this distress.

I argue that, like trauma, we're more familiar with constant distress than we might think because we've become habituated to frequent, low levels of it. Having too many people to help, with too few resources and too little pay, in the numbers we need in a society that does not prioritize or value our clients is our daily joke. But sometimes, jokes point to a darker truth we're trying to manage. I think we all may be at risk of moral injury because we're constantly exposed to this stress. We're hearing about it more now, not because it's new, but because the pandemic created an acute, overwhelming crisis in our usual, familiar levels of distress, like a virus hitting an already-compromised immune system.

UNCERTAINTY DISTRESS

Uncertainty distress is related to constraint, but distinct. This is simply when we don't know what to do. Confusion may be a part of this, or it may be when we lack the skills, training, or support we know we need. During the pandemic, we faced challenges we had literally never thought of before.

Had you ever tried to make a face mask before the lockdown? I had not, and when I look back, I see that the makeshift ones we started with (one friend of mine just wore his hiking buff on his face) were good, creative tries—and completely useless.[28] I remember putting together an elaborate system for rotating groceries and packages on shelves in our garage, trying to quarantine everything for a given number of days before bringing them inside. It was frustrating to keep track of what had been sitting where and for how long, so after a while, we just quit doing it. Would it keep my family safe? Would we get sick? Was I doing *anything* the right way? Did it matter? I quite literally had no idea, and instructions changed frequently as scientists scrambled to catch up. We didn't know what to do, and the people we usually looked to for answers didn't know either.

THE UNDOING OF OUR CHARACTERS

Jonathan Shay's brilliant *Achilles in Vietnam*[29] talks about a very specific injury done to soldiers, but some of the ideas also fit for helpers who are unable to help in the ways they believe they must. We'll start with the social contract for helping.

Shay talks about the experiences of soldiers in Vietnam (every war is unique, and all wars are the same). He describes what scholars define as *themis*, or what is right, orderly, and expected in your culture. Soldiers, he argues, can expect certain treatment and rewards from the people they fight to protect (money, honor, spoils from fallen enemies, etc.), and when that agreement is broken, there is a deep sense of injustice and outrage. While Vietnam vets coming home to protests and hostility instead of parades may seem like a far reach from the average human services provider in the 2020s, consider what helpers are "promised." If you are a helper, you are likely to earn little money and even less prestige—but you are promised that people will see you as noble, selfless, a "good person." What happens when that is taken away from you? Some frontline workers and many hospital staff saw that perception change over a breathlessly short time, from "clap-outs" at the beginning of the pandemic to threats and attacks as people grew more entrenched in their anti-vaccine or anti-mask stances. Doctors and nurses also felt a deep sense of betrayal when people lauded their dedication on the one hand but, on the other, refused to take the health measures that would keep them out of overflowing hospitals. "Help us to help you; we're drowning," said one health care provider after another.

This frustration is hardly new, however. For decades, health providers have felt some of the same betrayal from administrations that seemed more intent on profit than on patient care. I suspect we will see waves of people leaving medical work, and the pandemic may have simply been the last insult that sent them out the door.[30]

Shay uses this same mantle of justice and power for his book about the war in Vietnam: The solders he treated for trauma felt that indignant wrath when "agreements" were broken—with the military, with the Vietnamese guerilla fighters who, in the soldiers' view, failed to follow the "rules" of war, and with civilians who scorned them when they returned. Like the doctors and nurses of the pandemic, the soldiers said in essence: "We kept up our end of the deal. We did the unthinkably hard thing, and you did not give us what we deserve—*what you promised us*—in return."

Shay calls this failure of obligation "the first, primary trauma" of the veterans.[31] I think this idea, vastly different in scale, applies to helpers as well. We agree to see what most other people choose to look away from: the insidious, daily damage done to disenfranchised people, the wounds of abuse and neglect that fester for years, the grimy, discouraging ugliness of impoverished places. We see broken people, some of whom turn right around to break others. We helpers have agreed to clean up the mess society leaves. What is owed to us in this arrangement?

One way to think about this is in terms of *role* and *reward*: I agree to play the role of "helper." You agree that you will give me the materials needed to do this (funding for agencies, training in school, etc.). When I feel that you aren't holding up your end of the bargain by failing to make it possible to do what my role requires, I feel let down or even betrayed—like a soldier sent to battle without weapons to fight it.

Now let's talk about reward: As a helper, I probably didn't expect much money in return, but I did expect other rewards. These might include honor, respect, protection, or authority. For example, doctors and health policy officials received a lot of anger and even violent threats during the lockdown, and that is not usually the case.[32] This anger extends to other fields as well.

Social workers, for example, are sometimes portrayed in movies and on TV as the skilled, compassionate professionals we try to be, but we're just as likely to be the heartless bureaucrat dragging sobbing children away, or the insensitive jerk giving the hero a hard time when they try to adopt a baby. In these scenarios, "foster care" is usually a phrase invoked as a threat, a dramatic plot twist, or just the worst thing that could ever happen to a child, instead of the lifesaving option social workers sometimes have to use.

This, too, is a form of betrayal. If we thought we would be rewarded for our hard work by being seen as noble and helpful, and we're portrayed as villains or fools instead, then society has broken its agreement with us.

According to the ancient Greeks, this creates betrayed feelings of divine wrath (*metis*) or even madness.

And when that trust is broken, the result is not just anger or resentment, but sometimes uncertainty and even despair. What is the right way to do my work? If the people meant to equip, appreciate, and reward me cannot be trusted to do so, then who am I serving, and for what? Does my distrust now make the people I serve the enemy? If they are the enemy, who am I? Where am I safe? This uncertainty can create intense feelings of anger, pain, and isolation.

It's little wonder, then, that people suffering from moral injury struggle with "civilian" relationships as they find fewer safe connections there. For some, our work group, hospital ward, platoon, precinct, crisis shelter, or agency is the only place we feel safe and connected to anything or anyone.

In combat, four clusters of traumatic war experience can lead to moral injury.[33] These are in order of strongest to weakest, but there isn't much difference between the strongest and the weakest on this list; they're similar in impact. As I have throughout this chapter, I distinguish among the extremes of war while pointing out parallels to the helpers' exposure to suffering and destruction.

First is ***exposure to abusive violence***. We covered this in the previous chapter, so I won't repeat it here. I just want to highlight again how damaging it is for us humans to be witnesses to horror and pain, even if we ourselves are not experiencing it directly.

The second is ***deprivation***. The starving, freezing soldiers at Valley Forge or in the Battle of the Bulge in World War II are far more dramatic examples than the deprivation of staff at a hospital or social service agency. I want to point out, though, that some frontline staff may be grappling to stay above the poverty line themselves. Even when our own families are financially stable, the struggle to find resources for our clients can make us feel like we live in our own cold trenches.

Exposure to combat is another stark example in the experiences of soldiers or first responders, but it is present in the lives of other helpers, too. Some of us are literal neighbors to gun violence, gang, or drug activity.

Finally, the ***loss of meaning and control.*** Control means the ability to affect your surroundings, in this case, and meaning is derived, for us, from seeing the results of those efforts. This entire book discusses these wounds in one way or another.

When humans are exposed to too many of these things too directly, or for too long, the damage can, at its worst, be hard to heal. As Shay writes: "Severe, prolonged traumatization can bring wholesale destruction of desire, of the will to exist, and to have a future. Betrayal of what's right is particularly destructive to a sense of continuity of the value in ideals, ambition, things, and activities."[34]

Survivors of this kind of prolonged stress can't remember the value of things, are much more likely to be divorced, homeless, or unemployed, live in isolation, and feel suicidal.

SIGNS OF MORAL INJURY—CLASSIC DEFINITIONS

"What did *they* know about it?"

—Tim O'Brien, *The Things They Carried*

Some elements of combat moral injury are specific to that experience. But even in a quick list of symptoms, helpers may see themselves. We'll discuss each of these in turn:

1. Us-and-Them Mentality
2. Black-and-White Thinking
3. Inability to Trust Outside the Group, Form or Maintain Relationships Outside
4. Grief That Is Delayed, Denied, or Devalued
5. Use of Mind-Altering Substances

1. Us-and-Them Mentality

Negative feelings are highly mobilizing.[35] They are attractive compared to feeling powerless, and many of us cultivate a sense of righteous indignation—not just as a natural reaction to seeing suffering or injustice, but as a way to keep going, fighting against overwhelm and eventually, despair. Like jet fuel, it burns just as hotly, then burns out. It leaves us feeling depleted when we experience it too long, too often.

The bigger problem, though, is even more insidious: the us-and-them problem. It's not much of a leap to go from feeling solidarity against troublesome kids to grouping them all into one category. *All kids are a pain.* They are convicted as obnoxious before a trial, simply by virtue of being our client. The neglectful, abusive parents? Well, now it's *all* parents. Children's services will *always* let us down, administrators will always get it wrong. It didn't take me long to see the dismaying results of this view of the world. It creates cynical, confrontational, or apathetic staff and unjust treatment of our clients and partners.

2. Black-and-White Thinking

You could say that the main problem of us-and-them is that it simplifies things too much. Many kids *are* reachable, many parents care, and most child protective workers try hard (in nearly impossible jobs). Not only are the baddies not really the baddies[36], but we, "the goodies," mess up all the time too. Very few people are all-good or all-bad, omni-competent or useless. A way to describe this lack of nuance is black-and-white thinking. In *The Way Through*, I talk about the many snares and deadfalls of this type of thinking. It leads to power struggles, digging in, anger, resentment, disengagement, and just bad work.

Black-and-white thinking evolved to help us with simple problems, such as "That tiger is going to kill me if I run toward it, so I should run away from it." Toward = *eaten by a tiger*; away = *not eaten by a tiger*. Pretty straightforward. *Tiger/not-tiger* is the most boiled-down version of a problem you could face, and your brain will usually get it right. However, modern life is almost never that simple. Context, extenuating factors, multiple outcomes, and creative solutions to problems all require much more than *tiger/not-tiger* from us.

3. Inability to Trust Outside the Group, Form or Maintain Relationships Outside

What we lose when we lose the capacity to see others as valuable, equal, and worthy of compassion is too long to go into here—it could be its own book. To be honest, I don't think I could write anything as heartbreaking and instructive as a quick look around will give you. The world is full of stories about what happens when we forget that the people outside our little group are not always out to get us.

I think this quote from *The Myth of Normal* sums up nicely how the factors specifically involved in moral injury are, beyond doubt, a form of trauma. "My own observations of myself and others have led me to endorse fully what a review of the stress literature concluded, namely that psychological factors such as uncertainty, conflict, lack of control, and lack of information are considered the most stressful stimuli."[37]

4. Grief That Is Delayed, Denied, or Devalued

This is not a book about soldiers; it's not really even a chapter about soldiers. But to stay with our template for moral injury, we know that soldiers desperately try to forget their feelings, especially the sorrow and brokenness that may lie beneath rage. It is counterintuitive, but we have known for millennia that men and women returning from war need time and space to tell their stories, and to feel and honor their pain. Battle sagas told around a fire for generations probably started as catharsis for the people who lived the story. But telling the story must include a context for understanding, honoring, and healing, for seeing a way forward to rejoin the community. Otherwise, it can become robotic repetition—a sterile loop that precludes change and growth and even deepens the trauma.

Helpers, medical workers, frontline staff, and first responders tend to huddle among their own and exchange their "war stories," safe in the certainty that they will not be judged or questioned for the rawest tale, the ugliest emotions. Like the soldier, judgment would feel simultaneously agonizing and alienating for them. Thus, outsiders are not welcome. The trap here is that the safety may be bought at the cost of guidance or help. It's hard to save someone who is drowning when you are still in the water yourself.

So, it may feel safer to be among your own, but you may also find that you're in an echo chamber. The anger and pain you vent come back at you from someone else, and the echoes amplify in that small space. In my own small way, I have experienced the grim satisfaction of a good gripe session with my peers. I can complain with the best of them, and it can be compelling to hear others support your version of things. But usually, I felt worse at the end of these gripe sessions, not better. This is not to say that we should never do that. I think it's human nature to gather with like-minded people to vent, seek confirmation, and receive support. But whether it is a personal journey of recovery or something a group undertakes together, simply rehashing pain with no balm, no new understanding or skill, no challenge to damaging beliefs, cannot heal us.

We have to risk doing the thing we don't want to do. We have to move closer to the pain and actually work to understand ourselves and the specific nature of our injury. We usually need help to do this. But anyone who works with soldiers will confirm what Shay outlines in his wise book: You have to get to the grief. "Long-term obstruction of grief and failing to communalize it can imprison a person in endless swinging between rage and emotional deadness as a permanent way of being in the world."[38]

Again, he's talking about the unique heartbreak and rage of soldiers in wartime, but I'm going to hazard a guess that it's not so far away from the experience of helpers in the "war" of the pandemic. We shared some of this grief with the whole world and then had to put ours aside to witness it in others.

Did you have a chance to recognize and grieve clients who were lost or colleagues who had to leave due to the strain? Who handled staff departures, and how were they replaced? In a knowledgeable, caring way, or with little or no regard for the gaps (in skill, in experience) left by that worker? Forget pep talks and gift cards. When a loss is downplayed, unconsidered, or even ignored completely, it communicates with terrible power the truth about how valued the remaining staff are, and how important, or unimportant, their work really is.

In the 2025 medical drama *The Pitt,*[39] the lead character "Dr. Robby" works a grueling 15-hour day in an overrun Pittsburgh emergency department. As we get to know him, we see flashbacks to the recent death of his beloved mentor from COVID-19. The loss was so catastrophic that he apparently had to be away from work for a while, and now his colleagues watch him anxiously and ask how he's doing—clearly an unusual thing in this troop of battle-toughened doctors, nurses, and staff who scoff at any suggestion that they cannot handle stress. As the season unfolds, we see that the "the work goes on" attitude is both a refuge for Robby and a trap. He can't neatly turn off his grief and horror anymore, and it begins to undermine not just his care for patients but his own well-being. We get the sense that while the death of his mentor *was* recognized at the time, the loss simply hasn't been acknowledged enough for Robby.

I have worked in agencies where some staff departures were celebrated—with pizza and sheet cake and embarrassing anecdotes—and others were not. If a staff person left under a cloud of cynicism or complaint about the agency or had to be fired, a cloak of official silence dropped over the whole thing. It was spoken of as little as possible, and at times, it felt as if the person was simply erased from existence, like Photoshopping someone out of a picture after an ugly breakup. The excuse leadership gave for this weird, uncomfortable secrecy was often "confidentiality."

I have come to believe that this was a mistake. I should issue a disclaimer here: I'm not a human resources expert, and I understand that sometimes labor laws or liability issues for the agency have to be taken into account. Having said that, I think that even with those valid considerations, we leaders are often serving our own emotional discomfort and calling it privacy when we lock it all down and act as if nothing happened. No, I don't think everybody needs to hear all the gory details of the fireable offense or the angry exit interview or whatever other unpleasantness was involved. I'm not suggesting gossip or trash-talk. But I do think that it can be dangerously naive for managers and leaders to underestimate how sad, angry, or worried people might be in the aftermath of a sudden departure.

I learned as a manager that I had to talk about the loss—not the details specific to Employee A who left, but the feelings and concerns specific to Employees B through Z who remain. If people think, "That person got fired just for disagreeing," I want to disabuse them of that idea. I can do that by explaining that no one has, or will be, fired for that. If people are scared, "Oh my God, are they just not caring about keeping staff?!" I can talk about what we're doing to attract and keep people. If someone worries, "Will I be next?" I would gently ask, "Are you doing anything that you think might get you fired? Let's talk about that."

If staff liked that person and will miss them, it doesn't matter if I personally couldn't wait to get them out the door—I still have to give people a chance to talk about their sadness. I may need to listen to straight talk from staff about their resentment or anger now that they have yet another burden while they take up the slack caused by the departure. All these feelings are real and valid, and we ignore them at our cost.

Even when someone leaves without official action like a termination, I think stress and crisis make us think we can ignore all the "extras," like support after a departure. In a later chapter, I talk about the profound meaning of ritual—even when it's just a farewell balloon and a grocery store cake. When we don't recognize and celebrate and mourn a change, we tell our staff (and ourselves) that people just don't matter that much. That's the message soldiers can get from their leaders—and that is part of how moral injury is inflicted.

We have to create work cultures where feelings are seen as strength, not as weakness, and human frailty is supported and not punished. I am struck again and again by the taboos about expressing emotion in so many of our fields. My clients who are medical professionals talk matter-of-factly about the damage done to their reputation when colleagues see them cry. One highly respected medical professional that I treated was terrified that his depression and suicidal thoughts would threaten his career and even put his license at risk if anyone found out. It took months for me to gently persuade him to try a course of antidepressants because that prescription could be discovered in his medical record.[40] What kind of help is that for the helper? None at all. You're on your own.

5. Use of Mind-Altering Substances

We discuss this in more detail in later chapters of the book, but I want to address the issue here, too. When pain is too much, we humans instinctively and relentlessly seek relief. When we are seeking too much, too often, there is an injury there that needs to be treated and healed. Substance use issues among helping professionals can be especially insidious since other people—and we ourselves—assume that we "know better." Having to acknowledge a substance problem can feel humiliating for anyone, but the loss of professional stature (and real repercussions such as suspended licenses or other consequences) can keep us from getting the help we need.

CHARACTER IS NOT ALWAYS DESTINY: THE LIE DISNEY TELLS US

One of the most devastating things a human can lose is the belief that with a good heart and hard work (or pluck, or courage, or the-friends-we-make-along-the-way), things will all work out. We're encouraged to believe this from the time we are very little, in an infinite array of stories, movies, and songs. It's a lovely way to grow up, believing in yourself. Unfortunately, it's not always true. It's a wrenching loss to find out that some things go badly, and we may behave badly or fail to act the way we know we should, no matter how hard we try and despite being a good person. It can be especially hard for helpers to come to terms with this. If a doctor can lose the will to treat patients or a soldier can lose faith in flag and country, what protection do I have? Shay calls this "proving the lie of 'indestructible character'"[41] and believes that disillusionment and fear may make such losses unbearable for helpers to hear. How much harder is it for healers to recognize and face in ourselves? If my dedication has limits, or if I decide I can't or don't want to do this anymore, am I still a good person? We can feel robbed and broken if that capacity seems to have left us, without a clear way to get it back.

I've talked to my students about one of the pitfalls of being a helping professional, and I wrote about it in *The Way Through* as well. It is the evergreen lure of "knowing the answer." I think I've pointed out a time or two that human beings really do not care for uncertainty. It deeply freaks us out. We prefer knowing—or at least looking like we know. We can trace this right back to tigers: I want to know where the tiger is, so I know which direction to run to get away from it! We can't be too mad at ourselves that we find *knowing* irresistibly attractive.

When you are a helping professional, however, *knowing* ripples out farther. *Knowing what to do* means knowing how to help—which is your entire job. *Not-knowing* may mean failing at the least and causing harm at the worst.

We try to do no harm. The uncertainty distress in moral injury comes when I no longer know the right thing to do. This threatens not only our view of ourselves as smart, skilled helpers (and this is a central view of ourselves for most of us) but also takes us into the nightmare scenarios of doing damage or causing hurt, of making it worse instead of better. Most of us can tolerate that uncertainty for brief moments, but we need to feel that if we don't have the answer now, we can find it quickly. If the uncertainty is fleeting and rare, we can take it in stride as just another part of the job. But what happens when no one knows, and this not-knowing goes on and on? What happens when literally the whole world, its leaders and its doctors and its experts, do not know what to do next? Global anxiety is what happens. Helpers during COVID-19 experienced a double dose of this anxiety because the not-knowing quickly bled into work as well. How do we do home-based workers care for 3-year-olds over Zoom? How do we ask medical staff to wear tight masks for 18 hours straight? How do we keep our medically fragile residents safe while they're crying to see their families? How do I support my stressed staff when I feel like I'm drowning in fear myself? We didn't have answers, and we had no one to turn to who did. And at times, the stakes were literally life or death: Do we expose residents to a life-threatening virus, or leave them unstaffed to come to potentially life-threatening harm? Uncertainty distress went from an occasional hazard of the job to a constant, wrenching dilemma for many of us, and we may have felt that our "good characters" let us down.

The good helpers I know tend to rail against their own limits: not enough hours in the day, not able to single-handedly lift a client above crushing societal oppression, not psychic enough to predict the terrible thing someone did.

But it's worse than missing the nobility of our (inherently flawed) efforts to help our fellow human beings. Those who are pushed beyond their limits sometimes experience themselves as godlike, or at the other end, unfit to be among other human beings. Again, as is true of much in this chapter, other professions are more likely to experience the extremes I'm describing here, and ours sometimes catch only a quick glimpse of them.

Having said that, I have seen those among us who boast about needing less, doing more, and at times, thinking we know better than anyone else. I have seen law enforcement officers who believe they, and not the legal system, mete out justice, punishment, and reward and sometimes wander into a no-man's land outside of the rules. Shay and others write about the terrors of finding yourself this far from what is human and familiar, no matter how exalting it can be. Being an animal or a god cuts you off from human community. It alienates us from decent behavior and social or professional norms. The therapist who is intent on "saving" the client and then ends up sleeping with them may have started by telling himself he knew better than anyone else what was needed. This may not be so far away from the officer who has seen too much, felt too much, and reacts in a way far beyond her training or the limits of her authority. *What was going through his mind?* We ask in those situations, when it is too late, and the terrible thing has been done. *Why couldn't she stop herself?*

So many, many times, the person who, dazed by where they have found themselves or outraged that mortals are questioning their acts, will say an oddly similar thing: "I had no choice." What might be truer is to say, "I no longer felt any restraint." They had abandoned, or were abandoned by, a system they felt was too broken or corrupt to support them, or too inadequate to provide them with the tools they needed. "Restraint is always in part the cognitive attention to multiple possibilities in a situation. When all restraint is lost, the cognitive universe is simplified to a single focus."[42]

In its most severe form, returning to how things were is not possible. This may be because many factors are converging at once, such as inadequate support and the severity of the damage to the sense of self. We know that long-term stress from traumatic or moral injuries can create brain changes, such as an enlarged amygdala or shrunken prefrontal cortex, that can be hard to undo.[43] As with many of my clients, even after time and healing, life stressors can still trigger symptoms of moral injury like suicidality, feelings of isolation, deep shame, and self-loathing or anger at those perceived to still be in the circle of human society.

In *Trauma and the Soul*,[44] depth psychologist Donald Kalsched writes about a universal element of childhood trauma. He explores the feeling that innocence has been lost—and not in the usual way of experiencing the world one step at a time, protected by adults as we gradually mature and adjust, but brutally, suddenly, and completely. Moral injury, at its worst, can create that same aching loss of innocence, though adults may use words like *hope, optimism, faith in humanity*, and so on.

What might this look like in helpers? A useful example of the results of moral injury in helpers is the Moral Injury Symptom Scale—Healthcare Professionals version (MISS-HP).[45] In this inventory, manifestations of moral injury include:

Betrayal

This might be betrayal from someone specific, particular management or organizations, or the breaking of the social contract.

Guilt

"I didn't do enough, I didn't work hard enough, I can't care as much as I used to . . . " and on and on.

Shame

"I am a bad person," either from a lack of action or from an action that harmed someone.

Moral Concerns

"It's not clear what the 'right thing' is anymore, in this complex system. I don't know if anyone is really good; everyone just hurts someone else."

Loss of Trust

"People are lying, deceitful, or self-interested, and the world is always dangerous and bad."

Loss of Meaning

"There is no point to the things that I thought were good and helpful, and nothing can be done. My life's purpose doesn't exist."

Unforgiveness

"I will not forgive (specific people); society in general; myself."

Self-Condemnation

"I am too tainted, broken, or failed. I cannot be helped or cleansed from what I have seen or participated in or failed to stop."

Feeling Punished by God

"God is angry at me."

Loss of Religious Faith

"I used to be comforted by my faith, but now I feel there is no God, no universal force for good, no moral arc of the universe. I am alone."

HEALING IS ALWAYS POSSIBLE

Like the more familiar forms of trauma, moral injuries can heal. Medication to treat symptoms of anxiety or depression, skilled therapy, and communal therapy and support will help. I think that community is particularly important for these survivors because, more than any other kind of injury or loss, moral injury, at its core, is a community injury. Feeling that you no longer deserve to be around "decent" people, or that systems of ethics or faith have failed you, or are irreparably broken, keeps you out of the human society. Finding groups that understand, relate to, and support your pain is a critical element of care. Eventually, that circle may widen to include family, non-survivor friends, local communities, and perhaps faith institutions.

Human beings *cannot* survive without one another, and so healing requires that reconnection. We'll talk about ritual later in this book and use some simple forms of it as a wide lens for making sense of the world. However, some researchers have identified cultural and religious rituals, often from indigenous or Eastern traditions, that have helped heal moral injury in traumatized soldiers.[46]

Meaningful work is potent medicine as well. Projects that help soldiers with PTSD and moral injury find creative ways to contribute the skills and discipline they learned in their military experience. Operation Nightingale, a Ministry of Defence program in the United Kingdom, offers soldiers in trauma recovery the opportunity to work on archaeological sites.[47] Some of the highly specialized skills soldiers bring include carefully reconnoitering sites for tiny clues of an unexploded device, now used to spot minute evidence of ancient habitation. Finding and honoring the graves of past warriors creates a connection that spans centuries, as they protect the treasures of their culture and benefit their community. This is just one example of how the foundational elements of healing—connection, camaraderie, meaning, growth, protecting and serving others—can be found in a thousand guises, but all with the same power.

Identifying the values we still hold, or want to rediscover, can help us find our way back to ourselves. Gentry and Dietz offer exercises to name and list the values that are central to us, and encourage us to write a "code of honor" to prioritize what is most important to us as moral, ethical people.[48] In another example of reconnecting with our moral selves, we can take the values we hold most dear and examine the specific pain that results when they are violated.[49] Rather than focusing exclusively on the pain, we can sit with the values underneath it. It's paradoxical, but our pain actually tells us we are still moral beings at heart. Without those values and ethics, we would not be in distress when they have been broken. This, I think, is a lovely reminder of who we really are, no matter how far we feel like we've gone into the dark.

I will point out one last thing from Shay's book about soldiers. He learned through years of clinical work that the kinds of wounds these soldiers presented had to be healed in community; that is, in part by having the soldiers connect to other soldiers. They told their stories with the aim of healing and moving forward, not just trading and echoing pain. Shay called this communal work of storytelling and careful listening "the sacred stuff."[50] They could affirm their heartbreak and rage and work together to encourage one another to heal and move forward into the world. Crucially, they reflected to one another their humanity. For soldiers who sometimes felt like beasts and sometimes like gods, this was balm to their wounded moral selves.

As helpers, whether we feel we have been let down (sometimes) or that we have failed (usually), we have to find our sacred stuff, our ways to reaffirm our own humanity: fallible, worthy of care, valued for our existence, not just for our work. At the end of this book, I'll talk more about the other side of Kalsched's description of the loss of innocence, that within the traumatized psyche there remains the incorruptible, true self, the *soul*, as Kalsched[51] eventually calls it. For now, I'll say that in his and other therapists' experience, including mine, that part of ourselves, however damaged or inaccessible it feels, cannot be destroyed. It can never be truly lost to us.

PART ONE

Safety and Stabilization

I talked in the introduction about using Judith Herman's arc of trauma healing to organize some of the chapters of this book into three sections. This chapter starts our conversation about how we heal, so in this first section, we look at the task of Safety and Stabilization. We explore how to keep ourselves safer from empathetic distress and empathetic injury over time. In chapters four and five, we talk about changing how we define and view problems and how to sit with intense emotion.

CHAPTER THREE

The Three Empathies: Cognitive, Emotional, and Compassionate Empathy

"It is both a blessing
And a curse
To feel everything
So very deeply."

—David Jones, *In Parenthesis*

If I had a chance to sit down and talk with the readers of this book, I think we'd find we have a lot in common. Mostly, if I asked you how you came to be doing the work that you do, you'd probably tell me that you heard the same things I did when I was growing up: "You're such a good listener!" Or "I like telling you my problems," or maybe "You are so good with people!" If we tried to wrap all of that up into a description of your personality, chances are you'd describe yourself as empathetic. That's usually considered a great compliment, especially for women. In fact, for many of us, and I certainly would have included myself in this until recently, empathy is a central part of our image of ourselves. We care, we feel, we help, we contribute. And there's nothing wrong with that, as far as it goes. The problem is that research is telling us that empathy, as we usually think of it, may actually be hurting us.[52] And we may need to redefine what empathy is to save ourselves from distress, burnout, and, in some cases, serious damage.

In order to understand this, let's talk about the common definition of empathy: the ability to feel the emotions of others. When I was in graduate school, empathy was the goal. *Sympathy,* we were taught, is merely feeling sorry for someone's plight, but *empathy* is when we truly understand because we feel what they feel. And that, we were told next, is what would make us more effective as social workers— less distanced, more engaged, more informed about our clients' needs. However, recent brain science is supporting what the professional helper may have suspected for some time now: empathy is also a risk factor for burnout and compassion fatigue. If you read studies about those problems, you'll sometimes see shorthand or euphemisms: "emotional wear-and-tear" is a common one.

FACTORS OF BURNOUT

In this book, I won't cover how organizations contribute to burnout or how they can change that. My business partner, Kevin Aldridge, will discuss all of that in his upcoming book on how organizations can cause—and prevent—burnout among their employees.[53] For now, I'll just talk about some of the work factors that, over time, can turn the personal experiences of vicarious trauma, secondary traumatic stress, and moral injury into a bigger problem: burnout.

Like other definitions in this book, the meaning of burnout can vary depending on who you ask. The World Health Organization calls burnout "a syndrome conceptualized as resulting from chronic work-place stress that has not been successfully managed. It is character-ized by three dimensions: Feelings of energy depletion or exhaustion; increased mental distance from one's job, or feelings of negativism or cynicism related to one's job; and reduced professional efficacy."[54]

When we assess for burnout, these are some of the common factors (and you'll notice how much they overlap with the symptoms in chapters one and two):[55]

- High self-expectation/perfectionism
- Strong desire or need for recognition
- Neglecting or suppressing own needs
- Work is the only meaningful activity
- Lack of substantive social life

Even though I'm not discussing organizational issues, here are some of the indicators for work groups at risk for burnout:

- Times of high pressure (increased demand, after an MUI, during a review, etc.)
- Negative work environment (exclusion or bullying of some)
- Lack of control/investment in decision-making and problem-solving
- Poor organizational functions (communication, teamwork, clarity of roles, support, etc.)
- Isolation, lack of social outlet

To finish up this quick organizational check-in, here are workplace indicators for when an individual or group of employees might be in trouble managing their stress:

- Heavy use of leave time/PTO maxed out
- Decreased participation in team-based activities
- Increase in low-level quality issues
- Increased tardiness or absences
- No-shows

"Even the gainfully employed can experience blowback [compared to the stress of unemployment]. In a study of the British civil service, a lower ranking on the ladder of authority was a greater predictor of death from heart disease than commonly listed risk factors such as smoking, cholesterol, or hypertension." Australian studies found that a bad job is worse than unemployment.[56]

COMPASSION FATIGUE: AN OUTDATED TERM

I have never liked "compassion fatigue." It insulted me, and frankly, it scared me, too. When I heard it, I felt defensive at the very idea that I would someday just get "tired" of feeling compassion, as if I had just grown bored with caring about people. Of course, at the time, the phrase was meant to convey something like too-much-stress-for-too-long, like "metal fatigue" in an old building, and I knew that. But it still bothered me. As I said earlier, compassion is something I have prided myself on. It's my favorite quality. I think what was so scary was the idea that this capacity that I thought was at the heart of my nature could someday be depleted, damaged, or strained so much so that I would have to stop doing the work that, in some ways, defined me. The idea that I could end up entirely scooped out and hollow, deadened to feeling the pain of others, was terrifying. So, I disliked the term. In the research field on burnout, the phrase "compassion fatigue" is going out of fashion, thankfully. Our current language is both more accurate and, I think, more hopeful. Olga Klimecky, Dr. Tania Singer, and others[57] coined the term "empathetic distress," and I have expanded that to a broader idea of "empathetic injury." What I like about this phrase is that it describes what we now think is actually happening. We experience distress about the pain another person is feeling. This seems not only accurate but also much more generous. Humans don't like pain. It's human to feel distress when something hurts, not a failure, the way metal fails when it can no longer hold up a beam in a skyscraper. The hopefulness of calling something an empathetic injury is that injuries can heal. This is why I mentioned in my first book that, left to my own devices, I'm likely to call PTSD a traumatic injury rather than a disorder. It's a subtle distinction that matters only to me, maybe. But my ear catches the difference. So, like the other terms in the earlier chapters of this book, I'm going to talk about "compassion fatigue" using the language that makes sense to me. Don't worry about it if you see it named differently elsewhere. To discuss empathetic distress and the injuries that can result from prolonged exposure, we must understand what empathy is. Researchers believe that what we call "empathy" is actually three different brain states.[58] They're related, to be sure, but have distinct patterns that we can see and name.

THE THREE EMPATHIES

Cognitive Empathy

The first type of empathy is called cognitive empathy, and it's a good name, because it describes a state that is largely cerebral, not emotional. Using cognitive empathy, a person can observe and accurately label the feelings of another person but doesn't share them. Doctors, nurses, EMTs, and other medical professionals tend to be good at this kind of empathy, and that makes sense. Imagine a doctor at a hospital after a disaster has flooded her emergency room. She has to move quickly to triage patients, assessing levels of need and urgency. People are crying, screaming, or unconscious. If she stopped to *feel* the pain of each patient, she'd be incapacitated almost before she started. So, she glances at a writhing burn victim on a stretcher, assigns a level of severity, and orders the correct dose of pain meds—all without feeling much. Fun fact: This ability to recognize emotions in others without sharing them is also a quality we see in sociopaths. Many sociopaths (or psychopaths, depending on what you're dealing with and which terminology you prefer) have rather flat inner lives—they feel pleasure, anger, or boredom, but often not much else. However, they can be masters at recognizing and manipulating the feelings of other people. They can play on our fear or anxiety or pity, maybe mimicking those emotions to gain our sympathy and trust, all the while feeling just fine on the inside.[59] But back to helpers, whose problem is usually not a lack of empathy.

Emotional Empathy

Now we come to the empathy you are probably most familiar with—the one that the word "empathy" means to you. When we are in a state of emotional empathy, we can observe and accurately identify the feelings of others, but we also share them, at least to some degree. If I am emotionally empathetic, I wince or even weep at the pain of the people in that emergency room because I both *see and feel* their pain. When I was in graduate school, this type of empathy was the state we strived for. We took classes in mental disorders and, as social workers, learned about the experiences of immigrants, people of color, people living with chronic poverty and crime, or survivors of disasters, to sensitize us to the pain of people whose lives may be quite different from our own. This was all to the good. These lessons in empathy came with vague, occasional disclaimers to not feel "too much," lest you become burned out. How exactly we were to feel-pain-but-not-too-much was never explained, and so for me, burnout (and "compassion fatigue," as I discussed earlier) became an uneasy, mostly unmentioned fear as I started my career. This is not a slam on my profession or my education; other than some external factors of burnout, like workload, we didn't know much about the mechanics of this kind of emotional stress at the time. We were told to take care of ourselves and strive for "work-life balance," but again, this was rarely taught with useful understanding or tools.

And unfortunately, the quality of empathy that many of us prize most highly in ourselves seems to be a vehicle for our damage as well. Emotional empathy is great if, say, you're feeling my feelings while I'm celebrating my birthday with my family, enjoying presents and (lots of) cake. That's going to feel good to you. It's not so great for you if you're feeling my feelings while I am overwhelmed with terror as I relive an assault. Neuroscientists have spent the past several decades linking our reactions to the distress of others, finding that it creates similar levels of distress in us.[60] Let's go back to trauma. In *The Way Through*, I talk about the "window of tolerance,"[61] the range of activation that's normal for our individual nervous system. When we are in our "window," everything that is happening inside and outside of our bodies is expected, and our brains usually filter out most of it. If you are reading this sitting in a room where the temperature is in a normal range for you, you probably are not noticing the air on your skin or the hum when the air conditioning kicks in. It's something your nervous system has encountered before, and your brain is not concerned about a threat to survival, so it filters out the information, and you barely register it at all. Your heart rate is normal, your breathing is even, and your senses are focused on a task, such as reading, rather than frantically searching for escape routes. If something happens that is *not* in your window of tolerance (a loud noise, screaming from the next room, a burning smell), your nervous system will automatically kick into emergency gear: either the Four Fs for safety, or collapse and dissociation, for survival.

I'm sure you remember the "Four Fs," but in case you forgot, they are *fight, flight, freeze, and fawn.* I will use examples taken directly from nature: a human (me) vs. savage wildlife (the squirrels in my back yard).

Fight means any aggressive action toward the threat to make it go away. I have some very sassy squirrels sneaking up on my deck as I write this, moving in a loose pack like they're quietly overtaking a bunker in World War II. If I bang on the table with my water bottle and loudly shoo them away, eventually they slink off (throwing side-eye the whole way). I have been known to awkwardly throw things like car keys at them, so they know not to mess with me. (For any squirrel enthusiasts: Don't worry, my aim is terrible, the keys missed them completely, they have no fear of me whatsoever and mess with me all the time, and so the battle continues.)

Flight, of course, is the opposite: moving away from the threat to restore safety. In theory, this is what the squirrels are doing, scurrying away from me in terror. In reality, they are slowly moving the barest minimum distance away, complaining loudly and sulking like teenagers.

Freeze is what the squirrels do when a hawk circles overhead. They stop chattering and crouch down motionless in the branches of trees.[62]

And finally, *fawning* is moving closer to the threat to neutralize it, but not with aggression, as in a fight. If I were to offer the squirrels some peanuts, invite them to relax in comfy chairs, and flatter them about how fluffy their tails look this summer, that would be fawning.

When we are trying to deal with a perceived threat, we go into one of the Four F's, but if they don't work or if the danger is immediately life-threatening, we may go into a state of collapse. Rather than the stiff vigilance of freezing, we go limp. Prey animals may reflexively go into a stupor, like a possum "playing dead." So, I guess if I ever become completely overrun by the squirrels, I might go into a state of collapse.[63]

As we talked about in the earlier chapters, as helpers, we may not be dealing with life-threatening stressors, although helpers have been assaulted and killed by people they were trying to assist (nurses tend to be in the highest risk groups, but social workers and therapists are not immune to this kind of violence). Instead, our secondary and vicarious trauma comes when we go into these states simply by witnessing or hearing about the traumas of others. Our body can't distinguish between the pain we experience directly and the pain we experience by imagining and emotionally connecting to someone else's wounds. This is what we used to call "compassion fatigue," or, to use the more accurate current research term, empathetic distress. When we suffer this distress badly enough, long enough, we suffer what I call *empathetic injury*. I think this is not only more accurate, but it also communicates more than mere "fatigue." We are not tired of compassion; we didn't get sick of it, like when you hear a pop song a few too many times. We did not become bored with it or jaded with repetition. We experienced *an injury*; we are wounded by the depth of our caring in the face of the immense suffering of the world.

This, to me, conveys better the profound dignity of our pain. I don't judge people who use the old term, but I will not use the words "compassion fatigue" again in my career.

Compassionate Empathy

Feeling little, feeling too much: this sounds like that ominous yet vague warning from graduate school. Fortunately, research is identifying a third option, one that may contain the best of each stance so far. We can relate to what it's like to be in someone's shoes without actually having to put a pebble in our own. That is *compassionate empathy*.

Compassionate empathy is a state of observing and labeling feelings accurately; we're not zoning out or removing ourselves from the pain or distress of others to protect ourselves. Cognitive and

Compassionate Empathy bookend the concepts of empathy, with C at the beginning and C at the end.

Next comes the warmth of emotional empathy—the urge to reduce the suffering that we see.

So far, this is familiar. But compassionate empathy is distinguished by an important third element: a continuous, visceral awareness of our separate individuality, different from that of the other person. One of the dangers of emotional empathy is a sort of melding, where we merge with the person across from us. This results in an oversized sense of responsibility: "Oh my God, I have to save this person!" Then we experience panic or reproach if we cannot: "If I studied more or cared more, I could save them," or fear that their problems are now ours: "What if *my* child gets sick?" As always, clinicians use multiple terms to describe this response. When it's a chronic state, it might be called enmeshment or co-dependence. A fleeting experience might be called engulfment or dissolving of boundaries. Here, we'll just call it *merging*: your neurological reactions and survival reflexes are firing mine. Your feelings are mine, your problems are mine, your well-being is mine (or in my hands to fix).

If this happens rarely and lasts for only a few seconds, there's probably no lasting harm. But like we see with "little t" traumas, the damage comes from the frequency and the lack of resources, not the enormity of a single event. And of course, more rarely (but not never), we see the other end of that spectrum—someone who experiences this kind of merging from encountering or hearing about a single catastrophic event. Soldiers who liberated concentration camps may not have had the chronic exposure to suffering that a therapist has, but that experience certainly caused distress.[64]

The awareness of self is critical. We talked in *The Way Through* about Dr. Stephen Porges's word *neuroception*[65] and how it pulls together three levels of awareness to make up our overall sense of ourselves. There's:

Proprioception: where my body is in space, my position and orientation

Interoception: what the feelings and sensations are inside my body

Exteroception: what sensory information is coming from outside my body

We begin with neuroception, and from there expand to a more existential awareness of self, what I sometimes call "my basic OK-ness." Yes, bad things could happen to me. But right now, I am not experiencing the abuse this person is telling me they experienced. My children are not sick with leukemia like this mother's child is sick. My children are OK. I am OK.

As helpers, focusing on ourselves can feel counterintuitive or even morally wrong. I was taught in graduate school all about how to understand the Other: the client, the patient, the individual, or whoever that I was there to serve. But little time was spent on teaching perception of self, except watching out for the biases a practitioner might bring into the room. Even then, the problem with bias, we were told, is mostly that it distorts our ability to accurately (and empathetically) understand *the other person*. That's an important lesson in itself, but once again, the idea that you, the helper, are 50% of the humanity in that therapy room goes unexamined. I think a secondary result of this—the first being that many of us have little capacity for tracking ourselves moment to moment in an interaction—is that we are inherently devalued. Our needs get shoved down the list in order to emphasize the needs of the client. Again, there's not much argument to be made with this on its face, but we helpers may start to weave this into our psyches: we matter less than the work we do.

OUR BRAINS KNOW THE DIFFERENCE

I've saved the most astonishing part of all this for last: The Three Empathies are not just names for different internal emotional states. In studies done using Functional Magnetic Resonance Imaging (FMRIs), which show patterns of real-time electrical activation in the brain, researchers saw three different patterns of activation. For example, Singer and Klimecki found that emotional empathy could be identified by activation of the insula and the anterior middle singulate cortex, while compassionate empathy saw an increase in activity in the medial orbitofrontal cortex and the ventral striatum.[66] In other words, your brain really does experience the different types of empathy in different areas of the brain. They are close together, and there is some overlap, but they are distinct. We need more research to be sure, but it looks like these empathetic states, and how we function when we are in them, really do exist independently of one another.

So, back to compassionate empathy. In order for me to inhabit, in my bones, my essential OK-ness, I have to pay attention to what I am thinking and feeling (self-awareness), and then I have to have some tools to do something about it (self-regulation). We're going to explore what it feels like to move into compassionate empathy, and then we'll look at tools to make that shift happen.

To shift into a state of compassionate empathy, we start by adding warmth. An open-hearted wish for the other's well-being. Caring. Many medical professionals practice compassionate empathy already. The word you might have skipped over is "wish," but I'd like to spend some time with it.

For me, this word brings something important along with it. "Wish" doesn't automatically exclude the possibility that I might be able to bring that well-being about for you, but it doesn't automatically mean that I will, either. Sometimes "wishing" is very far away from any action we can take. While this might sound impotent and futile (feelings we helpers *just hate*), it could be read as "hope." *My hope for you is that someday you will feel better.* Again, this doesn't have to mean that I can't do anything now; maybe, as a doctor, I can further that hope by treating your illness right now. But it might also mean that you will feel better years and miles away from me. Maybe what I do today will affect that outcome, maybe it won't. For me, the heart of that hope could also be called *faith*. Faith might mean that I can contribute to an outcome, like planting a seed. I likely won't be there when it blooms, but I know I've played a direct role in bringing that about. Or it might be something much, much harder. I might be holding onto nothing more than the sheer belief that someday you will feel better, even if there's not a damn thing I can contribute to it happening.

Believe me when I tell you that this is sometimes our work. When I sit with bereaved parents, it is a hard struggle not to be washed away with feelings of impotence and helplessness, because I promise you, I know of no intervention, no worksheet, no journal assignment, no breathing exercise that takes away even an ounce of that kind of agony.

However.

I do think that my presence alone can be useful. Sitting in my therapy room, even if no one is saying a word, can be an oasis for the grieving where nothing is demanded, a place of quiet witnessing. I think that this might help break up the soil a little for something to grow later, but if nothing else, I can offer rest. Nothing needs to be explained or justified or "handled" in that little time in our room together. I know this has value.

When I'm sitting with someone, holding that imaginary apple basket for them, sometimes the heaviest thing that basket contains is hope. Hope that this person, sobbing through the worst pain I can imagine, might someday draw a breath that doesn't hurt. That someday, they will experience joy, that over time life will crowd in around the pain and give them something else to look at sometimes. I can hold hope that there will be times when a memory of their child will give them a minute of smiling, rather than an hour of desolation.

A newly bereaved parent can't tolerate that kind of hope right now. It would scald them. In fact, many of my grieving clients describe feeling everything from numbness to nearly uncontrollable rage when some (certainly well-meaning) person tells them, "This too shall pass" or some such platitude. I never, ever mention the invisible apple basket I hold in my hands. I just sit there with it resting in my hands. And I never offer them an apple (advice for finding the "silver lining" or "giving it to God" or whatever). My job in that moment is to just be in the room and keep the apples for them, to sit with my abiding belief that they can heal. And some of them, someday, will reach toward the basket themselves. They'll spontaneously mention a moment of peace on a walk, or laughing at a movie, or delighting in the resemblance on a grandchild's face, without a day of crying afterward.

That, for me, is the faith carried in that "warm wish." A last word about this faith comes from a quote I love to use when teaching about how to be a therapist. It comes from the world of hospice, but to me, it speaks to all the helping professions. In *The American Book of Living and Dying*, Richard F. Groves and Henriette Klausner have a lovely passage: "Healing [spiritual] pain is about holy listening, not compulsive fixing."[67] I am grateful to them because this phrase has become such a touchstone for me. I use it with students and audiences whenever I can. For me, this is also the most elegant way I can describe the faith of compassionate empathy. Rather than frantically scrambling for a way to change how you feel, I will be present with you and with it. I will trust in the "evidence of things unseen"[68] that things can get better or that the pain you now feel can someday ease.

What does compassion feel like?

As I was learning about compassionate empathy and preparing early presentations, I was also teaching graduate courses at Ohio State University. As usual, I used my obliging students as test subjects to try to sort out exactly how we can know when we are experiencing compassion. We talked about it, and they offered a list that I think encompasses much of what compassion might be. Of course, your experience is unique to you, and it might be a little different than anything you see here, but I think my students gathered a wide range of sensations, feelings, and thoughts under the umbrella of "compassion."

Warmth

One young man described the sensation of actual, physical warmth spreading across his chest when he felt compassionate. You may notice a feeling of warmth, or in the way we often use the word, an emotional draw toward, liking of, or softness about someone.

Caring

This, as we've discussed, is tenderness, concern, and wishing good things for the person in front of us. I need to emphasize again to helpers: There is no sense of obligation that goes with this feeling of caring. We may or may not be able to act on this feeling, and we are not required to.

Hopefulness

The belief that things can get better for this person—whether or not we are a part of that happening.

Groundedness/Centeredness

Grounded in a body-sense of our own OK-ness. Trauma expert Bessel van der Kolk gave a typically Dutch, earthy answer when someone asked him what *grounded* really means: "It means that I know that my feet are on the floor and that my butt is in the chair." He's talking mostly about the absolute disorientation that reliving trauma can produce. So, he's really saying that groundedness is its opposite: "I can feel my body (I'm not in a state of collapse or dissociation) and I know when and where I am." For our purposes, I would add " . . . and my chair is not your chair." In other words, I know in my gut that I am not you, I am not experiencing your problems or injuries, and right now, I am OK, even though you are not.

A preliminary definition of centered, for helpers: I can feel my body; I know when and where I am; I know and feel that I am not you, and that I am OK.

Calm

This speaks for itself, but in the tighter definition of trauma work, I believe that calm refers to regulation. My heart rate is at its usual resting level, my skin feels comfortable (neither flushed nor clammy), and my thoughts are centered on the situation at hand.

The environment feels hospitable to me, and I can interact with others while keeping my boundaries intact yet flexible. We could say it yet another way: I'm in my window of tolerance, neither too activated (hyper-aroused) nor too shut-down (hypo-aroused).

Expansiveness

For me, this is where we start to see the qualities of compassion pointing us toward action. "Expansiveness" can mean a literal, physical shift in perception. Some people notice their field of vision seemingly widen (or conversely, they'll say they had "tunnel vision" or "saw red" when they were angry and dug in about something). They can actually see more around them. Other people will feel their bodies expand or lighten (maybe compared to the dull heaviness of collapse if something has triggered them). Mostly, though, expansiveness refers to an emotional and cognitive experience. We feel OK enough ourselves to include others in our concern. We can imagine more than one road ahead of us, maybe one where both views prevail if we're in a power struggle. When we're locked in conflict with someone, it can feel like a narrow bridge across a mountain crevasse; it's wide enough for one person only, and the other has to be tossed over the edge. Win/lose. And that, of course, usually adrenalizes us with anger, though we'll call it self-preservation. "Well, I'm certainly not going to be the one pushed off the bridge, so I guess it has to be you." Now anger, aggression, and fear dominate, unless we retreat and quit the field with passive-aggression in the form of apathy (quite the opposite of empathy, apathy is emotionless). "Do what you want; I don't care."

When we are in an expansive mood, we want to reach out and include others, not fight to exclude them. We feel there's enough space for everyone to win, and we don't worry that more-for-you means less-for me (in the bridge scenario, maybe we widen the bridge so there's enough room for us both). I could go on, but in practical terms, it means that I can consider more than one outcome. I can hear your suggestion and entertain it seriously (we take turns across the bridge) or get creative about a third way (to hell with this bridge;

let's hike around the mountain and then go get pie). Unsurprisingly, expansiveness leads to creative problem-solving and usually more effective outcomes than a rigid battle for control, where someone inevitably has to go tumbling into the ravine.

Curiosity

It's not a coincidence that "curiosity" comes right along with expansiveness; they're practically two halves of the same experience. In order for me to come up with the creative, expansive viewpoint that lets us find solutions beyond I-win/you-lose, I have to start with being curious about you. Why do you feel the way you do? What do things look like from where you're standing? From getting out of power struggles about bedtime to helping people escape from mind-controlling cults, we have to start with respectful, good-faith questions. When we ask in good faith (not baiting someone in order to score a point), we do a number of different things. First of all, we communicate that we understand their experience is different, but also that it is valid, even if we disagree with it. Second, we might actually learn something surprising. Sometimes getting curious leads me to change my mind and come around to their way of thinking. This cannot happen if I don't have some interest in what they think or see.

I think this is a lesson we never stop needing to learn. It is almost unfathomable to us, really, that the world is not exactly what *we* see and what *we* think. Taking someone else's perspective is so hard, so unnatural to us, that I have come to believe we need constant work and practice at it. No matter how good I get at doing this, it's still not consistently my first reaction to other people. Whatever reminds us to do this again, to learn the lesson again, is helpful not just in solving the problem in front of us at the moment but in growing into better human beings.

"Flow" and Timeless Focus

I talk about Flow a lot in a later chapter of this book, but I included it here briefly because it is a reliable indicator for me that I'm in a compassionate stance. Like "holy listening," Flow means I'm focusing on what is happening minute-by-minute in the room—not how I'll write it up later, what I should have done to prepare before we started, or what I'm going to have for lunch. If Flow is available to you in your best moments in your work, you'll recognize it. If it isn't, you might need to do different work.

Patience

When we don't feel pressured to fix it, change it, stop it, or achieve it, but can just let what is happening in the room happen at its own pace, we have access to patience. As with curiosity, I can never learn this lesson too many times: It makes no sense for me to demand that people do things on my timeline when I cannot do things on anyone else's. I know in my own life that my growth, my healing, my learning, and my development all came according to their own clock. I believe in working hard, but I also know that some of the most important, internal processes of being and becoming have their own time. I some-times refer to "psychic time" with clients—not psychic like ESP, but in the sense of the *psyche*, the mind and the soul. Psychic time has no regard for the calendar. When you re-experience the sweetness of a memory or the stab of grief years after a loss, time does not exist. This understanding also helps me with my patience, but I still have to work on it a lot. Most of all, I have to work on cultivating patience with myself, and I try to offer this to my clients too.

Confidence

This is the gathering of all the things we've talked about so far. In the *X2: X-Men United*[69] movie (apologies, DC people), the villain Magneto leaves his clear plastic prison cell, which is suspended hundreds of feet in the air, by simply walking onto metal plates that materialize and float up one by one under his feet. What strikes me about that scene is how smoothly and serenely the actor Ian McKellen moved, not even glancing down to check if the next shining steppingstone was waiting for him. He just trusted it was there, and it was. I could spin this nerdy reference into a whole thing about comparing our abilities to superpowers, but I will rein myself in and simply say that when I have confidence that I can move from emotional empathy to a state of compassionate empathy, the process of helping and healing is clearer. I may not see the next move, but that is OK. I will find it when I need it, and so for now I can walk forward with confidence, stepping into thin air.

Moving into Compassionate Empathy: A Loving-Kindness Meditation

How we shift from emotional empathy to compassionate empathy is the next obvious question. As I talk about in *The Way Through*, this is really two steps. The first is self-awareness, recognizing the state you are in. The neuroception I explained earlier in this chapter sums up the constant communication with our own sensations, feelings, and thoughts. The second is having a tool or technique to move yourself out of one state into another.[70] I'm going to talk briefly here about a quick mindfulness exercise of moving us from one empathy (emotional) to another (compassionate). In a study, they had participants learn and practice a loving-kindness meditation, and that's a common term for it, although it exists in many versions in many languages and traditions around the world. I was given a simple version of this exercise, also called "Maitri practice" in Tibetan Buddhist tradition, by Shastri Janice Glowski.[71] I would not have presumed to engage in this level of teaching without guidance and permission. Here's how I teach this to clients, students, and audiences:

Begin in a comfortable seated position, in a room free from loud noises or intrusive interruptions. Allow your gaze to rest on a spot a comfortable distance away from you and maintain a "soft gaze" or simply close your eyes, whichever is more comfortable. Allow yourself a moment to get settled and check in with your sensations, feelings, and thoughts. As you do this practice, notice your experiences non-judgmentally, including if you get distracted. If you become anxious or emotionally uncomfortable, allow yourself to continue or to stop and resume later—each choice is equally valid and helpful.

Begin by viewing yourself with gentleness and kindness. Set an intention to maintain this gentleness with yourself during this practice. Connect with your felt experience in this moment and let go of commentary about "good" or "bad" thoughts, feelings, or sensations. You can choose variations in these phrases to fit you best. Pause after each statement for a moment, and let yourself connect to it, then move on to the next one.

Say quietly out loud, or to yourself in your head:

May I have happiness and the causes of happiness.

May I be free from fear.

May I be free from danger.

May I be free from physical harm.

If I do experience physical harm, may I be free from physical suffering.

If I do experience physical suffering, may I be free from emotional suffering.

May I be free from harm.
May I be free from danger.
May I be free from fear.
May I have happiness and the causes of happiness.

Now turn your attention to someone else. They can be in the room with you, and you can hold them lightly in your peripheral awareness, or you can visualize someone. If you are visualizing, imagine the presence of someone you really love. See their face and have a sense of their whole being. Whether you are working with a partner or a loved one you are thinking about, connect to a sense of holding them in gentleness and kindness. If visualizing is helpful, you may imagine them in a cloud of healing light or wrapped in protective angels' wings, whatever picture is most effective for you.

Go through the practice with these statements. Pause after each statement for a moment and let yourself connect to it, then move on to the next one:

May you have happiness and the causes of happiness.
May you be free from fear.
May you be free from danger.
May you be free from physical harm.
If you do experience physical harm, may you be free from physical suffering.
If you do experience physical suffering, may you be free from emotional suffering.
May you be free from harm.
May you be free from danger.
May you be free from fear.
May you have happiness and the causes of happiness.

Sit for a moment with these intentions, connecting to them. Check in with any sensations, feelings, or thoughts that may arise, without judgment.

In the traditional Maitri practice, you would then imagine the face of someone you feel pleasant about, then someone you feel neutral about, and then someone with whom you have difficulty, and then maybe the worst person you can think of. All with the same intentions. Finally, extend the intentions out to all sentient beings in the universe.

Then, let all of the practice go, and rest in the present without any purpose but to be in it. Notice that right now, there is nothing for you to do, or accomplish, or "fix," or achieve, or buy. Nothing to be added or subtracted. The moment has all it needs, and is complete. Rest and notice that completeness.

When I teach this to groups, I always ask them two questions afterward. The first is to simply pause and notice their neuroceptive state—how they are sensing, feeling, and thinking in this moment. Usually, audience members will report some change, that they are feeling calmer, slower, more relaxed. The second question is, "Which part was easier? Setting those intentions for yourself, or for someone else?" Invariably, there's a chorus of people saying, "Easier to do it for someone else!" I think this is the case for helpers generally, but especially for women: In our culture, we are taught early and often that to be a good person, you have to put others first. It's a hard habit of thought to break, and I don't expect that doing this meditation a few times magically erases decades of programming. Still, like everything we've talked about regarding the brain, we know that repeating this kind of focus on yourself really does make it easier over time. We can learn to put protecting and nurturing ourselves first. Not only does nothing bad happen, but it also makes us better at helping and protecting others. Dozens of studies, big and small, have been published examining the effects of mindfulness training, including shifting brain focus to compassion, on medical professionals, and while various experiments have produced stronger or weaker results, a meta-review of the data indicates that factors like executive functioning and situational awareness—two key skills needed for patient care—significantly improved even under highly stressful situations.[72] I predict that as more research is done, these outcomes will be consistent and provide important insight for how we train in the medical professions.

I believe there are probably many meditations or visualizations that can help shift our brain state from emotional to compassionate empathy, just as there are many forms of gentle movement and observation that can be grounding and healing. Over time, more studies will show whether that is true. I think that, as important as that research will hopefully turn out to be, it's not as important as you looking inside, noticing the empathetic state you are in, and then shifting it if you need to. With practice, you'll find the affirmation, prayer, or breath techniques that work best for you.

One last lesson I've learned about this: No matter how skilled, how seasoned, or how sensitive, every practitioner of healing work moves into those states sometimes. We feel flooded and merged with a client's pain or frantic and defensive, trying to imagine a magical solution we think we are supposed to have. I know I still experience those states all the time. The difference that skill and training make is the practice of noticing what's happening inside me, being gentle with myself about it, and then moving myself to a different place. I think that's why I always use the word "stance," because you can move your feet from overwhelming emotional empathy and stand in compassion. It's a decision and an action, not a constant state of being. We are not and do not claim to be perfected beings. Maybe that understanding and forgiveness for ourselves is the beginning of self-compassion, and when we have compassion for ourselves, then we can offer it and teach it to others.

CHAPTER FOUR

Strong Like an Oak, Strong Like a Willow: Changing What a "Problem" Is

"Gentle and yielding is the principle of life."

—Tao De Ching, 76

Safety and Stabilization continue here as we look at how we interpret stress and what we tell ourselves about problems. Learning to redefine what a "problem" is and what we can expect from life can reduce our pain and the agitation we feel to solve things. As we feel less pain and agitation, we may start to feel more stable.

When I taught graduate school, one of my favorite courses was also the one that drove me crazy. The Body Mind Spirit Social Work course integrated Eastern and Western approaches in clinical social work. Like all the courses Ohio State assigned me, it had already been developed, with a syllabus written by a professor. In that class, I taught from a textbook edited by that same professor, to which I would later add a chapter for the online second edition.[73] We got to talk about fascinating elements of traditional Chinese medicine like acupuncture, Tai Chi, and how the principles of Yin and Yang can be used to consider mental and emotional imbalance. *But also*, as with all the courses assigned to me, I immediately set about shifting things around in the lectures, deciding for myself what I actually wanted to talk about.[74]

As much as I loved this class, it was challenging. First of all, "Eastern" is such a broad word for dozens of distinct cultures, rising and falling over centuries—it's hilariously oversimplistic. "Western" isn't much better. And so, every semester or two, I'd struggle through, rewriting my lecture notes and trying to convey something about how two very different traditions of looking at and understanding people could be put together.

I think maybe the biggest shift for students was the way the authors of the textbook described an Eastern approach to thinking about problems. In the West, we tend to see problems as bad things, obstacles to happiness that need to be removed. I think we carry with us a mostly unconscious belief that if we could just clear away all these problems, once and for all, the rest of our lives will be smooth sailing, with clear skin, a full bank account, and happiness ever after. The truth is that I still believe this on some level, and I know that this idealized notion affects my stress. I get exasperated when it's just-one-damn-thing-after-another. When will everything be sorted out perfectly, forever?! I think that in my mind, it's like finally having a completely tidy and organized closet—and then you shut the door and never use it again. Which, of course, defeats the purpose of a closet. You might as well not have it at all. If I'm going to use that closet, I can learn some tidier habits, but it *will* get messy again, at least a little. Life and people and closets are imperfect.

I would describe (again, in a very simplified way) the Eastern approach as a more realistic view. In our textbook, client complaints were often referred to as "problems of living." I explained to my students two reasons why that resonated with me. First, it cuts directly through this weird wishful thinking that somehow, we can have our lives perfectly easy and figured out, and so problems can and should be removed forever. Secondly—and this was important to me—it took the negativity (and sometimes the pathology) out of problems. Problems of living, or POLs as we called them in class, were simply a side effect of being a living human being. If you are alive, you will have problems. It's not necessarily because you're weak, or ill, or the universe itself has it out for you. Obviously, some problems are grievous—terrible, heartbreaking problems like trauma, loss, and the devastation that man and nature can unleash on the innocent without warning. Some things are literally pathological, and some problems are really symptoms. For instance, the paranoid delusions of someone suffering from schizophrenia are obviously "problematic," in the sense that they're anything from inconvenient to terrifying, disrupting even the most basic aspects of daily life. They are *symptoms of an illness,* however, and if the illness is treated, then with a bit of luck, the symptoms (and the "problems" they stir up) will subside or disappear. This matters in a clinical sense that we don't have to worry about here. Everything not in the first two categories falls into the third one—problems from being alive. There are catastrophes, there are symptoms, and then there are problems of living.

How do we approach the problems of life? Do we treat each one as that last obstacle to everlasting happiness? If that's what you choose, you set up two struggles for yourself. First, the stakes are immediately raised. If this is the last thing standing between me and a life of ease and contentment, I'm going to be upset if I can't solve it. In fact, I may be "holding my breath" until this is dealt with and I can "finally relax." I hear myself saying those exact words regularly, to myself or anyone around me: "Ah, at last, it's Friday (substitute: laundry is done; notes are finished; that terrible meeting is over with, whatever) and so now I can *finally relax.*" As if not allowing myself to relax before now motivated me to get the tasks done, or more distressingly, as if relaxing is a luxury and I have to earn it. Or a third option: I want my relaxing to be *perfect*, with no nagging thoughts of what I have to do after the relaxing is over, so I scurry to get everything sorted to fully allow/experience/enjoy my rest.

Well. If I have to wait and get problems "fixed" before I can experience any of that, then I'm going to get *extremely* focused on the fixing, wouldn't you say? And if something seems to be a barrier, such as another person, or more often, my own disappointing self (I didn't actually get all the laundry done!), I might feel anything from annoyance to rage. This loop is tired and familiar to me and, I suspect, to many of you. This is the *problems-are-unusual-and-should-not-be-happening* impediment to rest, relaxation, and joy; the belief that bad or hard things in my life should not exist. If we see problems that way, then, of course, they must be gotten rid of, and eventually, like dandelions in your yard, you can pull them all up by the roots and banish them forever. Sounds appealing, right?

The catch is that you can never really get rid of the dandelions. Even if you do the backbreaking work of yanking each one out of the ground, seeds always blow from someone else's yard (probably mine, because the truth is, I refuse to weed my dandelions. I think they're pretty, and bees love them). You'd have to camp out in your yard all day and all night, never sleeping, always vigilant, obsessively monitoring the breeze for a single floating dandelion seed—and that way lies madness. But as light as my example is meant to be, there's a melancholy underneath the silliness. We do think this way, many of us, and we do stand out in our imaginary yards, shaking our fists at the wind and running around pulling up weeds. How exhausting, and how sad.

But if we think of some problems as just a part of living, our approach begins to shift. We can start with the understanding that, yep, if I decide to pull up the dandelions, I'm going to have to do it over and over. That might be OK with me! Maybe, in fact, I can find some sort of enjoyment in being outside, appreciating the deep-gold stain and the peppery scent that cling to my fingers after weeding dandelion heads. As I write this, that sounds kind of nice, actually. Suddenly, the "problem" has become an occupation, an exercise—even a meditation. Not every problem will yield such sensory pleasures, of course, but the point remains. And even simpler than that is to decide to chill out about the dandelion issue entirely.

Even the problems that are terrible and scary will look less threatening when we understand that problems of one kind or another will always return, so we'd better make friends with some of them. This doesn't mean pretending to love them or saying your shoe doesn't pinch when it does. It's more like greeting an annoying neighbor— you may slide out of this conversation faster than the last time, but there's really no hurry, because you *will* run into them again.

To switch images, I imagine us spending our lives on a boat, sailing on a wide sea. You don't have to be a sailor to know that on some days, the water will be nice and flat; on many days, the water will be choppy and sloshy, and on some days, there will be terrible storms. It's absurd to imagine even for a second that you will somehow be able to control the water and make it lie flat when you tell it to. No, obviously, the answer is you have to make your boat as sturdy as possible and learn as many sailing skills as you can. This image is close to how we talked about the philosophies of the East—specifically, Taoism and its later iteration, Buddhism.

The point here is not to sell you on these traditions (as it was not the point of the class, either). It is to say that in this sense, we in the West might benefit from looking at things through those lenses.

Briefly, the "law of dependent origination" in Buddhist thought says that all things arise from something else. Nothing ends or begins; it just changes.[75] There is no banishing problems forever, because they rise and fall, interconnected with every other experience of living. It would be like sitting in your boat and looking across the water. You see a wave, and you think, "Ugh! I can't stand that wave. I'm going to get rid of it, and then I'll never have to deal with waves again!" Well, guess what? *The water makes the waves.* The water *is* the waves. So, while the next wave may be more to your liking—bigger, or smaller, or more green-blue and less blue-green than the last one—there will always, always be waves. When you begin to accept this, you can take your eyes off the waves for a bit and instead look at your boat—i.e., the things you can control. And it also takes you out of the mindset of waiting for the waves—the things you cannot control—to stop happening. When you accept the nature of the ocean, you stop thinking about the waves.

This is a very long way of saying, "There will always be problems. If you are alive, you have problems." So maybe don't yell at them, or yourself, or life, when they crop up. It's part of being alive. The thing to consider is, how do I want to meet this particular problem, if it really is one?

Now we're talking about strength.

STRONG LIKE AN OAK, STRONG LIKE A WILLOW

What happens to oak trees on a windy day? Not much, actually. Some leaves rustle, and maybe during a particularly strong gust, some of the upper branches might sway a little. The tree itself stands firmly; it seems sturdy enough to handle anything that comes at it. In that same strong breeze, though, a willow tree looks ridiculous. Its branches wave around crazily, and the delicate leaves are churning in the same air that seemed to leave the oak untouched. What a lame tree, we might think, especially compared to the oak tree that isn't giving an inch.

Now imagine a tornado. What happens to the oak? Chances are that big, rigid, and unyielding tree is going to be ripped right out of the ground. All that unbending strength is no help at all when the wind blows hard enough. The willow, on the other hand, flops to the ground over and over, lying almost flat, but when the wind stops, it springs back up, good as new—give or take a few twigs.

My point is that we think that strength is only one thing: often, it's some version of immovability. I will not acknowledge what is happening to me; I will stay strong. From an integrated perspective, it's more helpful to think that strength has different qualities at different times. Sometimes strength means resistance, like a sturdy oak tree. Sometimes it means bending almost to the ground, *going with* instead of *standing against.* Sometimes we have to take it all the way to weakness-as-strength.

I've been talking to audiences about burnout, empathetic distress, and moral injury for years now, using words like "nurturing" and "self-care." I've trotted out that old favorite about "putting your oxygen mask on first." I believed every word of what I was saying. But in December of 2020, after nine months of sessions, day after day, trying to reassure my clients when I was every bit as scared and exhausted as they were, I didn't have enough left for them. I usually take the last two weeks of December as my big vacation of the year. I spend the holiday at home with my family, doing no work at all (barring a serious client emergency). My clients are always gracious about this, even though the timing is less than ideal for them. During the holidays, instead of a break from therapy, I think many of them would like to *increase* their sessions or possibly have me move in for a few days to help wrangle their families and referee when someone runs to the kitchen in tears. But they understand, and I take the break knowing it will be enough to replenish me.

Not that year. By the time December started, I was already done. I was sleeping badly, eating too much, withdrawing from family (partly because I could not sit in front of a computer screen for One. More. FaceTime). I was numbing out by shopping online, playing games on my phone, or doom-scrolling late into the night, diagnosing myself first with COVID-19 and then with whatever other, more exotic diseases I could find. I was snappish and weepy. Even I could see that I was not doing well. So, I announced to my clients that I would be taking three weeks off instead of my usual two. I made this decision and immediately felt relief—for a minute. Then came the rush of guilt and second-guessing. *Is it really that bad? I could have sat through another week of sessions, even if I had to fake it a little. Maybe I'm really a selfish therapist, irresponsible, uncaring. Am I just lazy?* And on and on. It's both painful and dull to put it all down here, and I suspect many of you reading this can guess exactly how this talk went, because something like it plays in your head. Finally, I started telling myself what I'd been saying to my clients: Strong like an oak, strong like a willow. You need them both. I'd been strong-like-an-oak for months with my clients and family, being the reassuring presence who heard their fears, found some kind of action to take, and offered them the chance to put down some of their burden. But now that well inside me was filled up to the top with opaque, muddy water, and it needed time to settle and clear. I could have all the opinions I wanted about whether I *should* or *shouldn't* need the time, but my opinion didn't matter at all—I needed it, whether I liked it or not. So, I worked on letting myself be strong like a willow. I bent to the ground. I rested and retreated rather than talking much with relatives. I politely turned down virtual hangouts with friends, and I didn't jump on every group text. I did some modest holiday things, but I didn't try to include every-single-tradition and every-fun-thing. I let it be a small holiday rather than a lavish one, and I didn't shove myself or my family into the usual chores to Make Everything Perfect. Hardest of all, I let myself live with the possibility that my clients were disappointed or even stressed not to have access to me, while I did what I had to do to be well. It won't surprise you to hear that they were all supportive of my taking care of myself, just as I really knew they would be.

As I look at that time with some distance and perspective, I'm proud of myself. It was hard to embrace that thing I'd been urging on others: allowing weakness, allowing vulnerability, allowing "failure" in order to be OK. By the time I came back to my practice in early January, I did feel better, and while I may not have been a perky willow again (I was definitely missing more than a few leaves and twigs), I was ready to be available. I was breathing. I'd been weak-to-be-strong. In case this sounds overly inspiring, let me reassure you that I still struggle with the idea of disappointing anyone or failing to live up to their view of me as generous, giving, always-ready-to-help. But having done it once, when I really needed it, I know I can be strong like a willow again when I need it.

Accepting *what is* (we are born on a boat, we live our lives on the ocean, and the next storm will always come) with *what can be* (things can get better, your boat can be stronger, if you work at it) is so clearly, ridiculously contradictory and just plain nuts, that the only possible comparison is to light. How convenient, then, that light is the metaphor that carries this book! Without triggering some of you (including myself) with memories of high school science classes, I'll just remind you about one of the few things that I remember from physics—that light itself is impossible. The light that is shining on the page you are reading or beaming out from the screen with your e-book projected on it is not happening. It cannot happen. In all the years and all the decades scientists have experimented with light, it always shows itself to be two contradictory things at the same time: a particle (little bits of stuff) and a wave (moving energy). Now, obviously, that can't work; something can't be stuff and not-stuff at the same time. But here we are. As you might remember, this impossible thing is what quantum mechanics is all about. Quantum physics is just the study of things that are really, really big, like black holes, and really, really small, like the teeny bits of matter that make up an atom. Everything in the middle we can explain with good old regular Newtonian physics, but not the really big, the really small, and the completely impossible, like light. The goal of quantum physics is to figure out how it all fits together—sometimes called the Unified Theory of Everything. On that day, we will be able to fully understand why light is two mutually exclusive things at the same time. Hurray!

Weirdly, we humans have understood all of this from the beginning of time. When they announce the Unified Theory has been discovered and all the physicists can go home, they will find waiting for them:

- all the people who lost someone they love, and still love, and still grow and evolve with them, and who will live their whole lives with them, and yet know they are dead
- all the people who have loved and hated someone at the same moment
- all the people who doubt themselves and everything else and feel themselves pulled along by something that cannot be proven to exist
- all the people who know some problems cannot be solved and keep trying anyway
- all the people who cannot possibly go on and take the next step

In other words, these scientists will find the rest of humanity waiting there for them. The human intellect may struggle with the concepts of the universe, but the human heart has always been able to hold two opposing things at once. More than two, actually. Our hearts can contain everything. And this is how you can embody two different kinds of strength inside you at the same time: the strength to resist and the strength to let go. The strength to pride yourself on your acceptance of rest and retreat as much as you value your fighting spirit. The strength to be strong and the strength to be exhausted. So don't be afraid that you will be weak. Don't worry that the willow tree won't spring back up. Learning what kind of strength we need to embody at any given moment is a lifetime's work, but it's part of how we care for ourselves and model self-care to others.

There's an old saying that "calm seas make poor sailors." Going back to our ocean, we could say that moving with the currents and learning more than one way to handle our boat takes practice, but it will make us better sailors.

We wrap up Safety and Stabilization with the way we can process emotion rather than numbing it, overreacting to it, or pretending it doesn't exist—all the things that may *feel* safe and familiar but actually can cause us more trouble.

When emotion can be faced and welcomed, we may not feel the pull to numb out with behaviors or substances that tend to breed other safety issues while we're busy not feeling. Learning to tolerate intense emotion is a thread throughout all trauma work (and much of any other kind of therapy).

CHAPTER FIVE

Giving Your Feelings Wings: Tolerating Intense Emotions

"Emotion is the chief source of all becoming-conscious. There can be no transforming of darkness into light and of apathy into movement without emotion."

—Carl Jung, *Aspects of the Mother Archetype*

"Ahh, Borderline Personality Disorder—everybody's favorite!"

This is how I sometimes lightly introduce this diagnosis in presentations. Given its reputation and how it can sometimes be weaponized, I think some lightness is merited. Without going too far into this topic, I'll just say here that personality disorders are often argued about in mental health circles. They are notoriously hard to define, especially since there's still no solid agreement about what a personality is, or if it even exists. But I do like to mention Borderline Personality Disorder (BPD) when I talk about trauma, because many people with complex trauma histories seem to be diagnosed (often incorrectly) with this. It's the spooky diagnosis that brings shudders to audiences of mental health professionals, our own version of a horror story because some people who meet those criteria have been known to act in unbelievably destructive, manipulative ways. Staged suicide attempts, false accusations, frivolous malpractice lawsuits: severe BPD has it all. Borderline

Personality Disorder is considered one of the hardest disorders to treat, and many clinicians avoid it entirely.

So, what's a discussion about BPD doing in a book about burnout? Well, in one of the best discussions I have ever heard about BPD, a clinician suggested that we should rewrite this diagnosis entirely and rename it as an "emotional dysregulation disorder." I'll leave the conversation about the stigma of saying there's something wrong with someone's entire personality for another time, but I like this idea for other reasons, too. When you try to describe the real problem of BPD, it's helpful to think about two poles: At the first one, we have a broken emotional thermostat. I talk about this image briefly in my chapters about emotions in *The Way Through*, so I won't go through it in detail here. We'll just use the simple analogy that our emotional "temperature" is usually under our control, like the thermostat in a room. We can make small adjustments, turning the dial a little to calm down or cheer up, and there's a limit to how far up or down we usually go. We aren't often in a consuming rage or absolute bliss; we have a range of emotions that's normal for us. Hopefully, this is in line with where others are, too. We need to be in harmony with the emotional ranges of the people around us to function in society. In fact, one of the things that freaks people out about BPD is that when someone suffers from it, they can be disastrously out of range with everybody else. The person who bursts into angry tears at the first hint of opposition in an otherwise routine staff meeting is probably going to be in serious conflict with the norms of the group. This is why BPD can cause so many problems in the lives of the people who have it. For one thing, they get fired a lot.

The other "pole" is an unstable sense of self. People with BPD have trouble seeing themselves as consistently good, or worthy of love, or even as someone who really exists. This isn't the part we're going to be talking about here, but allow me a quick aside to plead for compassion: You can imagine how violent emotional storms + deep insecurities = desperate behavior. This is not to excuse the extremely inappropriate or harmful things people with BPD sometimes do; it's just a reminder about why they may be doing it.

Now, our business here is not BPD itself but to use it as a springboard for a conversation about how we understand and manage emotion, even intense or distasteful emotions. Dialectical Behavioral Therapy is usually called the "gold standard" of working with BPD, and we'll adapt some ideas here as we work on the emotional distress of empathetic injury.

Before we leave BPD entirely, though, I do want to make one more point. When a helper's sense of self is bound up too much in helping, what is usually stable in our self-esteem can start rocking dangerously if even helping is no longer possible, as we saw in its extreme form in Chapter Two about moral injury. I think this may contribute to some of the stigma of this diagnosis and that element is on us to fix.

With apologies to high-fidelity Dialectical Behavioral Therapy, I'm going to paraphrase some of the ideas and techniques they use with the most broken emotional thermostats. The first thing is to learn to look at emotions as signals, not problems. This is part of the discussion in *The Way Through*, but if you'll bear with me a minute, some of it is worth rehashing here. An emotion might be a signal of a problem, like pain in your jaw might be a signal of an infected tooth. So, when we feel an emotion, it's good to ask ourselves what it might be signaling. But it's just as important to remember that the *signal itself* is not necessarily the problem. In other words, we should first pay attention to the tooth, not the pain. This isn't to say that we shouldn't take the medicine or ice pack the dentist gives us; it's just that focusing only on the pain is to miss the point of it, especially if we numb it so effectively that we never get around to seeing the dentist at all, and that probably makes things worse in the long run.

Also, getting swept away into panic because of the pain keeps us helpless. A small example: When I was pregnant with my first son, we decided that I would have him at home without medication.[76] Once labor really kicked in, the pain was worse than I had ever imagined pain could be—and if you'll forgive the pun, I am a terrible baby about pain. I started to feel terrified and unable to focus. I remember exactly the moment that I had to go deep inside and have a firm talk with myself that I *could not* let myself freak out. I had to find a way to climb on top of the panic so that I did not become completely hysterical, unable to listen to the coaching of my birthing team, unable to push, unable to get myself and my baby through this. I had to find a way to interact with and ride the waves of pain without making it worse by panicking and telling myself ohmygodthisshouldnotbehappeningtome! In a strange way, I had to decide to be OK with what I was experiencing and concentrate instead on what I needed to do, or I would be lost.

While this is a dramatic comparison, I think it works. Sometimes our distress is as intense emotionally as that pain was intense physically, just as disorienting and panic-inducing. We have to find a way to interact with intense emotion.

The next idea I've borrowed from DBT is a slogan I've repeated to countless clients, and myself: "Just because you feel it, doesn't mean it's actually happening." This is another facet of pain-as-signal: Pain may be happening because of internal factors, instead of a reflection of something that's really happening in the outside world. In *The Way Through,* I use the example of someone saying something that hurts my feelings. Maybe they intended it, maybe they didn't—maybe I misheard them, and they didn't say it at all. It should be routine to take a minute and ask ourselves, "Is there any objective evidence that another person could see that this is actually happening? Or am I having this feeling separately from what is going on?" By the way, this is one reason why most human beings need some kind of connection with other human beings to fully mature: Marriage or other close partnerships offer so many chances to practice this! Is my spouse/partner/important person *really* attacking my character/parenting/value as a member of society? Or are they maybe just asking me to turn down the TV?

Take yourself through this reflection often enough, and despite your best intentions, you'll probably become more emotionally mature and self-aware. Ugh, growth. It's the worst.

Now the other side to this is that just because it's happening inside you doesn't mean it *isn't* happening outside, either. In other words, something inside is asking you simply to pay attention and find out more. There may not be anything you need to do outside of yourself (except turn down the TV), but there may absolutely be some comforting, nurturing, or self-talk needed now. In other words, inside stuff is no less important than outside stuff—it just helps to know what you're dealing with so that you can be effective. If it's an infected tooth, go to the dentist. If it's old feelings of shame, worthlessness, or fear, go inside yourself and deal with them. This is not about one being more relevant or important than the other, and of course, they're often closely related; they're just not the same. Pain-as-signal really could be understood to mean that the signal points in both directions, inside and out. You just have to figure out which way to go.

WINGS OF THE BIRD—EMBODYING EMOTION

Once you know what direction to turn, it helps to have some tools when you get there. In *The Way Through,* I write about the Golden

Square of attunement, attachment, attention, and adjustment. These are the stages we repeat over and over when we are interacting deeply with someone. I also explained the CALMER Skills and how they can help ground and orient us when we are pushed out of our Square, when we may be feeling unsafe and out of control. Here, I want to go further with techniques that can help with regulation and deep acceptance. I'll turn to the work of the rightly famous Tara Brach, an expert in trauma recovery and mindfulness. She's going to have more to say later about our chronic distractedness and the toll it takes, but for the moment, we're going to talk about her approach to working with powerful emotion. Her books, *Radical Acceptance* and *Radical Compassion,* offer many insights, a few of which we're going to use here.[77]

Brach explains this exercise to an audience by suggesting that we start with noticing where a sensation is in the body. In *The Way Through,* I talk a lot about how emotions are experiences that are located in the body; they're not thoughts, even though our thoughts and feelings can be so closely connected that they seem like the same thing. When I teach Brach's Wings of the Bird to my clients, frequently the sensation they notice first is tightness or pressure—often, but not always, in the chest or throat. Without jumping in to explain or diagnose it ("Oh, that's anxiety! It's because of . . ."), I just ask them what feeling, word, or phrase seems to go along with the sensation of that tightness. It might change (in fact, it almost certainly will), but we're just labeling it for now. I also encourage them to go with whatever words pop into their heads first, rather than getting distracted by trying to find just the perfect name for it. Being exactly accurate is much less important than the noticing itself, and I don't want to get us off track. My client might pause and then say, "It feels like fear." Brach's first "wing" is now in place. What is the sensation (Tightness), where it is in the body (Chest), and what name will we give it? (Fear).

Now for the second wing. Brach tells us to ask some variation of this question: Can you allow that Fear, that Tightness in your chest, to be there right now? As before, the emphasis is on the fact that it will not always be there, and sometimes I'll tell my client explicitly, "I'm not asking you to allow it to be there forever, just for right now." That usually feels like less of a commitment, especially when it is a feeling or sensation that's uncomfortable or unfamiliar. Brach suggests different ways to word the question, and I usually try a few of them so that my client can figure out which one they like best:

Can you say "yes" to this sensation/feeling right now?

Can you give permission to this sensation and feeling for now?

Can you make space for this sensation/feeling in your body for now?

This next part is important, and for me it is the embodiment of the compassion at the heart of this practice: It doesn't matter what the answer is. This is also the hardest thing for people to grasp. Most of us are conditioned to try to do well, to get the right answer, or to please the person working with us; this powerful instinct takes a while to unlearn. Clients usually think they know the answer they're "supposed" to give me, "Yes, I can allow . . .", etc. It takes lots of gentle reminding, but I always emphasize that their body may say no to the question! If I ask, "Can you give permission for . . . " whatever, and the first, gut-level answer that arises for you is "NO!," well, that is a perfectly good answer, and it is to be valued and protected as much as a "Yes." It can be pretty funny, actually. A client will tell me the answer is no, then quickly glance at me, worried that they're now in trouble for getting it wrong. The truth is, and this is why I love Brach's method, if we say we are going to be compassionate toward our feelings, then that has to mean we will be compassionate with *all* of them, not just the ones we like. Not just the ones we think might be acceptable to other people. So, a client might say, "Yes, I can make room for that feeling," and I say, "OK, what do you notice that comes up with that 'yes'?" If that instinctive, gut-level answer is "No," I say, "OK, what do you notice that comes up with that 'no'?" In other words, we do exactly the same thing regardless of the answer. They are both equally good. "I don't know" is another perfectly good answer, too. No matter what the answer is, the next step is another round of the same questions again. The first wing: What does that answer bring up in your body, and where is it? Then, what word or phrase best fits *that* right now? Sometimes I borrow Brach's wording and ask, "Where can you connect with that the most directly in your body?" Then the second wing: Can you give permission for this to be happening right now?

For this next round, I'll also point out that the sensation may have moved (let's say from the chest to the throat) and may be associated with a new emotion (let's say, sadness).

And so on. After a few rounds of this, clients become aware that the sensations and feelings in their bodies have subsided to a gentler version of ease or calm, at least to some degree. It can be hard to remember, but even though this more peaceful state usually feels like a relief, it's not actually the goal. The goal is what we've been doing to notice and then accept whatever is happening.

In my experience, when we take a minute to really notice embodied emotions and name them, and then at least consider the possibility of giving them "permission" to exist for the moment, things do seem to start moving. But that's not always the case, and certainly not always right away. More important by far is the message that we're not trying to suppress or get rid of the feeling—just accept and learn about it. And on the other side of the coin, we're also not saying Oh-I-love-this-feeling-so-much-I-hope-it-stays-forever! That's just too much to ask of anyone. Some feelings are mild or pleasant, but some are intense, and intensely painful. No human being would want those kinds of feelings all the time. But, and this never stops surprising me, even after years of this work, welcoming the tough feeling in, if only for a minute, seems to allow it to move on. I loved the name of the exercise, Wings of the Bird, partly because it beautifully conveys the "two parts of a whole" of noticing and accepting, but coincidentally, I had already been using the image of a bird in feeling-work in therapy. I would sometimes describe the process of "sitting with a feeling" as holding a bird cupped lightly in your two hands. You're not throwing the bird on the ground and yelling, "I hate you; get out of here!" In other words, you're not suppressing, raging, or arguing with the feeling, or trying to pretend you're not having it. But in our bird example, you're also not crushing it to your chest, saying, "I love you, you have to stay exactly like this forever and never leave!" You're not insisting on how you *should be* feeling, or that a pleasant feeling must never end. Both of those things—angrily hurling it to the ground or smooshing it against you forever—would be very bad for an actual bird, and it would also be a deeply weird way to behave. No, instead, you just let the bird rest lightly in your hands, maybe gently turning it this way and that to see it better, learn about it, and appreciate it—and eventually the bird will fly away. Maybe it will come back another time, maybe it won't. The point of this metaphor is not just that we can't get rid of or have a chokehold on our feelings, but also that their nature is to "fly away." Even more critical than *that* is the essential recognition that *we are not our feelings.* We are bigger than they are, and we can "hold them in our hands" and look at them while they last, but they don't comprise our total reality. They move through us; they do not become us. As I said, I discuss these ideas in *The Way Through,* but this is a good opportunity to take them a little further.

"Wise compassion" is another name for this exercise, and I like that almost as much as Wings of the Bird. The word "wisdom" doesn't imply that I know everything, or that I'm supposed to think my way out of my feelings. It just reminds me that I can engage my conscious mind alongside my feelings—that both can be operating at the same time. Here, I think it also means simple discernment: I feel this and not that. When you can give even the simplest language to an internal experience, it helps shrink it down a bit. Things start to feel understandable with language—and that helps us manage them.

Compassion, as I've talked about throughout this book, can mean acceptance or tenderness. We can be so harsh with ourselves about our feelings that a simple practice of asking where they are and what they are, and then allowing them to be whatever they are, is a profound practice. Every time I teach this technique, I get another chance to learn it again myself and practice it. Over time, I've noticed that I'm a little kinder, a little more patient with my sometimes-powerful feelings of anger, or frustration, or shame—and that's really just another way of saying I'm a little kinder with myself.

In Chapter Three, I talked about tools to help shift from emotional empathy into compassion when we are too merged, too overwhelmed with the feelings of the other. The loving-kindness meditation is one example that can be useful in changing the pattern in our brains. Wings of the Bird can be another, and as you find more, I believe you'll start to see that the elements are always the same. Look inside.

Be honest and gentle about what you see there. Use that gentleness to remind yourself that your essential nature is valuable and worthy of care, and that nature is bigger than whatever you are feeling right now. Remind yourself that your presence is helpful, and that sometimes, that is enough.

PART TWO

Mourning and Remembrance

In this section, we shift from Safety and Stabilization and move to deeper emotional work. In trauma therapy, the healing task of Mourning and Remembrance means looking at what was lost, stolen, and damaged as a result of the trauma. Feelings are tolerable (just barely), and sometimes, deeply feeling the emotions of anger, fear, and grief that were too overwhelming or outright dangerous at the time is possible now. Listening deeply to the self allows those experiences and emotions to come out. We'll continue this theme in Chapters Seven, Eight, and Nine.

Chapter Six

Graffiti of the Spirit World: Messages from Your True Self

"Even in the strictest environments, the authentic self fights to shine through."

—Steven Hassan, *Combating Cult Mind Control*

My sister is an accomplished installation artist. One of my favorites of her projects involved large wooden cutouts she'd made of secretarial shorthand words, then carefully painted with silvery, light-reflective materials. She attached these to the side of an abandoned house on an alley. As cars drove by at night, their headlights would hit and illuminate the reflective symbols, but once the car passed the house and the headlight beams shifted, the words went completely dark again, with no glow in the rearview mirror. The piece was titled *Graffiti of the Spirit World, 1994.*[78] She imagined that angels might write notes to one another this way, in a language we humans can't see and couldn't understand if we did. We would pass by these messages every day, unaware that they were right there in front of us, in giant, mysterious, shining script.

We have our own way of communicating with ourselves, and it might, at first, be just as hard to see and decipher as that angelic language. I've noticed in therapy that people often know things even when they don't want to know them. The cliché in movies is a therapist analyzing a client's dream. Truthfully, I love it when clients share dreams, and I think that sometimes our subconscious minds replay scary scenarios or reveal deep themes that way. But in my experience, we usually don't need such an indirect message to ourselves. The truth we know but may not be ready to admit is often right there in front of us. This knowing may come to the surface in jokes or in symptoms that seem to be related to something else entirely. It may be in what we dislike or fear in others, or in the themes that run through our minds when we get quiet. When people have experienced trauma, it can separate them from their own body-awareness, as we'll talk about more in Chapter Twelve. Intuition is linked to body-awareness, or neuroception. Our "sixth sense" may well be the combination of *all* of our senses put together in fractions of seconds, too quickly for us to consciously register. This may be part of the reason many trauma survivors seem not to have that "little voice" that warns them of bad situations. I believe the same thing can happen to helpers as well when we are overexposed to vicarious or secondary trauma. If we are habitually numbed or disconnected from our bodies to minimize feeling our clients' pain, we may not be able to hear that small voice of intuition when we need it.

In her book *Yes Please*,[79] actress Amy Poehler mentions that she is "obsessed" with *The Gift of Fear* by Gavin de Becker and tells all her friends to read it. Throughout *The Gift of Fear,* de Becker talks about listening to our instincts and intuition, and he uses examples of the levels of knowledge, from the faintest inkling all the way to outright terror.[80] One subtle level of this kind of awareness that has always interested me is humor and jokes. Earlier, I talked about the seasoned-veteran routine among helping professionals that impressed me so much as a young social worker, the world-weary, seen-it-all attitude

I tried to emulate. I mentioned that this approach may in fact mask cynicism and emotional distancing, both hallmarks of burnout. I think that another hallmark of burnout is the jokes that grizzled veterans tell, the "black humor" that can be heartless and shocking to outsiders.

I think this type of humor can serve many purposes. One, it identifies us as part of the group, being "in on the joke." There aren't many things more important to human beings than creating and maintaining an identity in the world, and being part of a group is a powerful way to do that. Identification and affiliation can be signaled by otherwise-obscure references we use with one another and by the shared experiences we laugh about, maybe mystifying the people outside our circle.

Jokes can defuse tension, build connection, and be a source of creative play between us. But de Becker's point is relevant here as well, which is that jokes can *also* be a way for us to express something we don't know yet, or rather, something that we're not quite ready to admit we know.

He tells the story of a bank office where a mysterious, elaborately wrapped and stamped package arrived one day. As the staff gathered around, wondering about it, the bank manager walked away to his office, joking that he was leaving "before that thing explodes." Seconds later, it did, killing one of the bank employees and badly injuring others. They were victims of the Unabomber. De Becker guesses that some of the clues about the package (no return sender, overly taped, too much postage) registered as anomalous: not strongly enough to make people's fear conscious or change anyone's behavior, but just enough for someone to make a joke. De Becker goes on to explore why we may kid about something we're not ready to confront or discomfort we don't quite know what to do with yet. I experienced this myself in a funny but disconcerting way on a vacation years ago.

My husband and I were staying in a small resort town while visiting family. We went to a local coffee shop and struck up a conversation with a friendly man in his early 50s sitting at the table next to us. He told us that he was a late-in-life, newly ordained priest. He had changed his direction in life after an entire career in business. We, of course, were fascinated to hear his story and the unusual path his life had taken, which he graciously shared with us.

Since I am a lifelong, enthusiastic extrovert, this is the kind of travel pastime that I just love. I collect new people the way other people collect souvenirs; learning about someone and maybe getting a glimpse into their life lets me experience a place I'm visiting more vibrantly than a map or tour guide. The truth is, striking up this kind of conversation with strangers is not hard for me. You can't be a social worker for 30-plus years and not develop the ability to get to know people quickly. I have a little craft and a little charm, and I ask questions that will usually get a person talking. My interest and friendliness are genuine, but there's a bit of intention mixed in as well. It's helpful to practice your skills. Of course, I try never to be intrusive or press people to talk about things that are too personal or too uncomfortable, but I can usually read the feelings and color of the conversation, and I have a good chance of directing it toward connection and sharing, even if only for a minute or two. Many people like a friendly chat, and I rarely have a negative interaction. That way, I have the pleasure of meeting interesting people (and everyone is interesting once you get to know them), and hopefully, they enjoy making a friend. I have to say, though, that this perception and skill in making new connections also gives me a sense of control, or at least a comfortable awareness about my skill in creating the interaction we're having and reading the person I'm talking to. It's embarrassing to admit, but all this also means that I can be taken quite by surprise when someone perceives something about *me* that I didn't know they could see, probably while I was busy directing the conversation and trying to learn about *them*.

In the conversation with this new priest, I made one of my standard jokes about how my husband and I did not choose lucrative careers. I must have said something else in that same vein a little later on because our new acquaintance said lightly, "You must be worried about money. You've mentioned it twice."

I was comically shocked—it's possible my mouth literally dropped open. *Excuse me?? Using my own therapist mojo on me without my knowing it? How very of you, sir!* At the same time, I had to laugh and admire his perception. Of course, he was right. While we certainly live more comfortably than a lot of people in this world, we don't have wide margins in our budget for things like vacations. The cost of this trip must have pushed past my emotional comfort, but so subtly that I hadn't really thought consciously about it. On some level, it bothered me enough to make jokes about it to relieve the stress, but not quite enough to rise to full conscious awareness. In the world of inner messages, the jokes were meant to release emotional pressure and maybe eventually draw my own attention to the source of that pressure.

Even more uncomfortably, I had to spend time with the idea that I may have missed all this because I'd been too busy enjoying the use of my ability in drawing him out to pay attention to *myself*—always a troublesome subject.[81] I've reflected on that priest's remark many times over the years since then, and even in writing this now, this small anecdote humbles me. The inconvenient gift he gave me was this reminder: Even someone who spends a lot of time observing their thoughts and feelings can miss something about themselves that might be obvious to even the most casual observer. Paying attention to our jokes and stories may tell us something we didn't quite realize about what we're feeling, pointing to a situation that is causing us more distress than we are ready to confront. And comfortably focusing on and subtly examining other people may be a way in which we helpers miss that message and fail to tend to our own issues. Now I listen carefully when someone makes a joke or throws off a little comment, even (and especially) me.

So far, these are relatively easy questions to ask ourselves: What do I really think or feel that might be hidden in the anecdotes I always seem to tell? What emotions of mine are making themselves known in unexpected ways, so that sometimes others see them before I do? As we look more deeply into this, we enter the realm of the shadow.

> Everyone carries a Shadow, and the less it is embodied in the individual's consciousness, the blacker and denser it is.
>
> —Carl Jung

The *shadow* used to be a term known mostly to depth psychologists and Jungian analysts, but now it's almost as common on social media as "mindfulness." As always, when something becomes widely popular, it can get stretched out to mean almost anything you want it to mean. The original Jungian construct was this: Inside the zone of our conscious awareness is our ego (how we see ourselves) and our persona (how we want other people to see us). Just outside that zone of awareness is the shadow.[82] Jung thought a lot about paired opposites, and he created a modern version of ancient concepts about the pairs of traits that we tend to lean toward in our personalities.[83] The terms Introvert and Extrovert are so familiar that I don't even need to explain them. The other pairs are commonly called Thinking vs. Feeling, Intuiting (information from the self) vs. Sensing (information from the world around you), and Judging (reaching conclusions to close a situation) vs. Perceiving (keeping processes open as much as possible). These terms came into popularity with the Myers-Briggs temperament sorter.[84] Personality inventories and sorting tools are always fascinating to human beings, which I think is why we've probably had some version of them since we have been human. Astrology, the Chinese zodiac, numerology, phrenology, the Enneagram—each system rises and falls in popularity according to the fashion of the time, but the lure of finding out more about ourselves never goes away.

Nevertheless, I don't follow clinical personality constructs like Myers-Briggs closely; over my career, I've observed that they are supported very loosely, if at all, by research, and most clinicians I know don't use them for serious diagnostic purposes. The "Big Five" personality traits in the acronym OCEAN (Openness, Conscientiousness, Extraversion, Agreeableness, and Neuroticism) seem to be enjoying some solid results in psychology research, but it's a long game.[85] Still, we keep looking for language to understand and quickly describe ourselves to others, so I think that at least culturally, these versions of self still have their uses. I think of them as mirrors, not X-rays.

How you react to the descriptions you're given can tell you more about what you want and fear about who you are than actually peering inside you and telling you something demonstrably real about your makeup. Someday, science may find a useful, detailed instrument that will accurately predict, based on your personality, what your reactions and experiences will be (after all, doctors use X-rays not out of idle curiosity or finding out everything that ever happened to you, but because when they want to know what to do next for you, right?). In the meantime, we have an informal language for talking about experiences, whether or not they accurately predict who we are across our lifespans.

Jung conceived the warring parts of the human psyche, drawing on Freud, his teacher and mentor. Eventually, Jung famously (for him) and bitterly (for Freud) broke with his teacher, and in the process developed his view of us as wanting more than merely to reach a bloody stalemate with our animalistic ids, craving sex and food and power, and our noble superegos, wanting to be virtuous and harmonious with society. Jung believed that our selves want wholeness above all.[86] This can mean a sense of completion, reaching the fullest potential we contain within ourselves for wisdom, connection, and action in our world. Wholeness also means that all the parts we are made up of can work as one being. This doesn't mean that every part of our psyche merges together into a single entity, like throwing ingredients into a blender to make one smoothie. A better way to think of it might be the Earth. The regions around the globe can be utterly different from one another—think the Pacific Ocean and the Sahara Desert—but each forms part of the single worldwide ecosystem. There is conflict at times, like when hot air from the desert hits the cooler temperatures over the ocean and creates violent storms, but they do not need to conquer each other. They coexist, though they sometimes clash when they meet. Jung would argue that the shadow cannot be conquered, nor should it be. It can only be known and respected.

This is where, in my opinion, some of the videos and soundbites about the shadow do a disservice. We cannot fix up the shadow and then blend it into ourselves like throwing an extra banana into that smoothie and watching it disappear into a creamy drink, completely incorporated and no longer a recognizable, separate thing. Your shadow is more like a wolf that lives in your basement.

So, let's imagine that somehow, for some strange reason, you have a wolf. If you lived in the middle of nowhere, this might be OK, but let's say in this example that you live around other people, in a city or town. Being a good citizen, you know that you can't just let the wolf run around the neighborhood biting people.[87] What happens if you ignore the wolf and pretend it isn't down there? Well, the wolf just gets louder and more insistent, doesn't it? It will howl and rage and claw at the basement door, and if it tears away at the door long enough, it will find its way out. By then, the wolf might be so starved and violent that it's impossible to manage, or so sneaky that it slips by without your noticing, and then it goes out and does a lot of damage. You can't make your wolf a pet and invite it upstairs with your family and guests—it cannot be tamed. It is not a dog. Even if it seems docile for a while, sooner or later, a wolf will be hard to control, and it will tear things up, snap its jaws, and make a terrible mess.

An alternative is to get to know your wolf. It has to stay in the basement, yes, but what if you go down the steps regularly to keep the basement well-lit and reasonably comfortable? You check in with the wolf, ask it what it wants, toss it some red meat, and show it understanding and kindness. Jung emphasized wholeness and balance, not fixing. This wholeness means the parts of ourselves that we like must live alongside the parts we don't, and we have to accept all of them, not just some of them. His point about the shadow is that it can't be made shiny and attractive, but we can't push it away, either. Our shadows are the unevolved, selfish, unhealed parts of us. The part that worries we won't get what we want and sneaks or lashes out to get it. The part we think is unattractive—or actually *is* unattractive—to others. Anger, fear, rage, and shame are all very familiar to our shadow, and in fact, many authors have pointed out over the years that every monster story is really a shadow story, and every villain has some feature we recognize in our own reflection in the mirror. Taken to its extreme, this can include things about ourselves that we feel (or have been told by others in our lives, our culture, or whatever) are monstrous and must be hidden. Any member of a persecuted group can relate in some way to the damage and self-loathing of this. For some of us, "coming out of [whatever] closet" is really "climbing up from the basement" and learning to see ourselves as completely human and not monsters at all. I should clarify that this kind of situation is not reconciling with your shadow, but distinguishing what is *your* shadow and what other people have *projected onto you from their own shadow selves*, driven by their own fear or judgment. Do not ever carry someone else's shadow for them, letting them tell you who you are. Our own shadows are responsibility enough.

Jung's pairs don't represent right and wrong. They can mean, more neutrally, big and small. Developed and underdeveloped. Known and unknown.[88] This can include weakness, such as in our nondominant hand. We use it less, so it has fewer neural connective maps in our brains, making that hand slower, weaker, and harder to control. It's not bad or wicked, of course, but that underdevelopment can hamper us. The weaker our nondominant hand is, the more it can become an issue in the right set of circumstances, and many athletes practice long, tedious hours to correct this and bring that lesser-used side into some sort of balance with the other.

In fact, every one of those pairs gives us the essential blueprint for the shadow. The extrovert in me is matched by a weaker, less-developed introverted side. Since I use (and often like) my extroverted side more, I'm more familiar with it. I can behave in extroverted ways and be conscious of doing so. I can use the skills I have built to leverage my extroversion in ways that benefit society (drawing out a shy client to help them talk through their problems) or to satisfy my own wishes in a socially acceptable way, like chatting up a stranger and getting a spontaneous lesson out of it, for example.

In our imaginary house, the one with the wolf in the basement, extroversion would be a welcome guest. It can sit comfortably in my living room and chat politely with others. But, like almost all humans, I have some traits or capacity for introversion too. Introversion is less dominant for me, so I know it less. It takes longer for me to recognize that my introverted self has emerged, and I need time to be alone and recharge. It may take me by surprise, and by the time I know I need that break, I've already snapped at someone or gotten bored and fidgety at a meeting that has gone too long. I'm less skilled and polite about working with my introverted side than I am with my extroverted self because introversion is less developed and less familiar to me. I feel less confident about navigating this side of me to get what I want and need in that moment. It's like taking your dog out for a walk vs. trying to put a collar and leash on a wolf. It takes a lot more effort, and you will probably get dragged around some.

Some parts of my shadow are pretty benign and can be dealt with using reasonable attention and discipline. For me, *thinking, sensing, and judging* are weaker areas. Jung would tell me that I might want to strengthen them, because when we're *very* unbalanced in one direction or another, we miss some skills we need. Systematic, analytical reasoning will never be my strong suit, but learning to be more comfortable researching and gathering information, or carefully building an argument link by link, is something I can get better at with practice. Eventually, I'll be more skilled and more comfortable with this sort of thinking, and I won't avoid that kind of work so intensely. That is a version of venturing down into the basement, tending to my wolf and helping it adjust, so this thing that will never be a major part of my psyche can still find a place.

The shadow even shows up on vacation. Getting slightly embarrassing feedback was uncomfortable, and I could have gotten defensive or dismissed his observation. Acknowledging that there might be something going on that I wasn't fully aware of took a bit of mental toughness on my part, a willingness to peer down into the basement to learn more about what was bothering me. I'm not saying this was the most searing soul-searching anyone ever did, but it is a good example of the small daily opportunities we have to look at and learn about our own shadow rather than diverting it into defensiveness, shameful secrets, or destructive behavior. Like most things in life, being willing to address the shadow becomes a habit, either way. We can routinely choose to look down into the basement to try to learn and make peace with those challenging parts of ourselves, or we can keep deciding to bolt the door more firmly instead.

So, our wolves are made up of scraps and odd bits, things we aren't comfortable with or avoid, things that get tossed into a basement. What happens when the wolf howls and scratches at the door depends on how big we've let it grow and how hard we've ignored the wolf we raised down there. People with rigid, black-or-white beliefs about good and bad people, or good and bad parts of themselves, tend to have savage wolves that do terrible damage when they get loose. Hateful bigotry, violent anger in response to insecurity, inability to tolerate failings in others, vengeful grudge-holding, and most of all, hypocrisy and lying, tend to be the hallmarks of that kind of wolf.

Fortunately, most of us will never harbor that much negativity in our psyches, but it's the paradox of wolf ownership that if you never really admit how ugly or unpleasant your wolf can potentially be, you are accidentally making it stronger and wilder. For me, I know my shadow is emerging when I take irrational dislikes to things or people and cannot see them in a fair and nuanced way. I can't take their perspective, and I angrily refuse to try. Chances are, there is something in that person or situation that reminds me of something I don't like about myself, or fear I am, whether that's true or not. I especially react negatively to arrogance, for example. It's not a big leap to figure out that I secretly (or not-so-secretly) worry that I can tend to arrogance and bossiness myself, and I find that fact embarrassing and unattractive, especially if it morphs into its uglier, more destructive cousin, self-righteousness. I don't think I have much of that extreme version, and it's not just a peculiar distaste I happen to have—I think most people would agree that smug self-righteousness is a bad trait. In other words, it's not unusual in itself that I don't like arrogant, self-serving, judgmental people, but some of my reaction may be fueled by my own worry that I might have a smidgen of it myself, even if it's in a milder form. I would rather spend a lot of time and energy condemning terrible self-righteousness in someone else, though, than trying to address my own occasional arrogance.[89]

When you're willing to really know your own wolf, it tends to settle down some, and it's less likely to sneak out and cause havoc without your realizing it. Our shadow will never be the same as the other parts of our psyche; we will probably never like it much, and we cannot sugarcoat it and pretend that we do. I will never especially like the parts of me that can be arrogant, judgy, or bossy. Wolves will never make good house pets. Luckily, that is not what we're trying to do when we are trying to listen intently to our inner selves—we're just trying to learn from that wolf, to take it seriously and hear what it has to tell us, so we can stay in balance and live in some kind of peace with it.

Some of you may have already made the links among uncomfortable truths, the darker regions of the shadow, and moral injury from Chapter Two. There can be a complex relationship among them. If you have been exposed to the most brutal parts of human nature, you might find that you have to tap into some of those darker parts yourself. It might be rage at one more intrusion on your work. It might be bitterness at people who don't see all the things you've seen. It might be self-pity if you struggle to find compassion in others for your pain. I use this term less judgmentally than it might sound. If, as children, we have been exposed to adults who pitied themselves rather than reasonably prioritized our emotional needs, we may learn that feeling sorry for ourselves is the only comfort we will get, and no one will be sad for us but ourselves. The problem is that when we are in that loop of sorrow, we may also remain in that childlike state of not knowing or believing we can take action on our own behalf to change something. That can leave us stuck, and the sorrow can curdle into self-indulgence or blame. That blame and pain can be deflected onto other people, and now the wolf is loose again.

I want to be exquisitely clear that this is not the same as holding people accountable for the actual pain and injury they may have caused us or are inflicting on others. I'm talking about when a reaction seems to be coming from somewhere other than what is happening. It can be hard to distinguish the shadow ("I screamed at that nurse because an underdeveloped part of me feels entitled to immediate attention from other people when I'm upset") from moral injury ("Working here has made me just as bad/mad/crazy as everyone else, so I might as well be my worst, angriest self. Maybe that's who I am now") or secondary traumas ("I screamed because I just can't take it any longer"). I think it's vitally important to think about using these examples as prompts to gently explore more.

It is my core belief that there is no part of us that is completely unacceptable or that deserves to be banished forever to exile and darkness. This is true whether it was always part of our psychic makeup—the shadow—or the cumulative result of too much pain, too much distress (secondary trauma), too much we've had to compromise, or things that we had to do to survive (moral injury). That "graffiti of the spirit world," that secret language from ourself to ourself, wants us to pay attention, to accept and to heal, not to judge or condemn. If your pain, your wounds, or your shadow are very deep, this work may be more than you can do on your own. I urge you to find a skilled and compassionate therapist to help you bring all the parts back out into the light. This won't make every part of us pretty or delightful, as I've said, but that's not the point. We don't need every part of ourselves to be tidied up and attractive to others, but we *do* need to be known and whole to ourselves. There are folktales around the world about what happens when someone tries to shake off or sever their own shadow, and how lost, empty, and miserable they are until it is restored to them. Peter Pan's adventures with the Darling children begin when he appears in their room and asks Wendy to sew his shadow back on. We could interpret his eternal boyhood, perhaps, as the lack of the self-awareness that the shadow demands we develop in order to be fully mature.

Other Languages

Learn the language you have for yourself. When we talked about jokes and the shadow, we talked about how observing our feelings and actions, our jokes and narratives, can tell us a lot. You can also look at how you work. Over the years, I've struggled with organization and staying on top of tasks I find unpleasant or boring, and I've told myself many negative stories about myself because I didn't match what I thought good people, smart people, or accomplished people do. But after enough repetitions of this endless cycle, I finally began to trust myself. I've learned that when it comes to a task that tends to pile up (*like clinical notes*), I need to make sure nothing gets so far out of hand so that I have more work than I want to do to climb on top of the pile. I injured my hand several years ago, and while it was healing, typing was difficult. I ended up with a months-long backlog of notes, even with the voice command program I was using, and it took a lot of time and effort to get caught up. That became a helpful guardrail to keep in mind: Don't get more than a few weeks behind on work, because it's a real pain to catch up. But unless something unusual like an injury gets in the way, my typical pattern of let-some-things-go-and-then-catch-up works well for my mind. Some weeks, I'll feel very motivated and keep everything tidy and current, and other weeks, some part of me seems to need to lie low and direct my energy to other things. Then I come back again to the busywork, energized and refreshed. Learning this pattern is a form of message from me to me: Trust that your rhythm works for you, even if it isn't how other people do things.

This level of listening includes our bodies as well. I write at length in *The Way Through* about how emotions are in the body, and how sometimes somatic clues like a flushed face, shaking voice, or nauseated stomach might tell us that we are feeling something, long before we recognize it in other ways. In a later chapter, I'll talk more about the work of Gabor Maté and what happens when we do not listen to the body until it is yelling at us. I talk about how stress may be affecting our body, how we can shift our relationship with it from constant judgment to something gentler, and how we can support its intrinsic strength. I also talk about issues that might emerge first in the body, like bingeing on food or using substances to shift our mood. I won't go into any of that deeply here, but I will tie this together by pointing out that our bodies can't lie to us. We use our minds to lie to ourselves and to other people; in fact, we do it all the time! But our body knows only what it feels, and there are no excuses or rationalizations that will fool it.

In *The Way Through*, I use body signals as a key to recognizing and identifying emotions. In fact, it was one of the Commandments of Feelings: Feelings are in the body.[90] I also point out that pain, fatigue, illness, tension, irritation, inflammation, or jumpiness can all be sending a coded message that something in our lives is out of balance. For a very mundane example, I tend to have neck and shoulder tension, and I know two things about it: First, I have to stretch regularly and get occasional massages or physical therapy to keep the tightness from developing into headaches and other problems. Second, it's made worse when I spend too much time looking down at my phone or my computer. So, when my neck gets painfully tight and the headaches start, I know two things because my body is telling me all about them; I am not doing what I need to do to take care of myself, and I am not looking up from my work, my preoccupation, or even my distractions. I literally need to take a break, lift my head, and look at other things. I need a different perspective. You'll notice that I've moved from a concrete thing (my neck and shoulders are too tight) to a much bigger message about my life (stop obsessing, look around, be here). The languages we use can be subtle, but the messages can be simple and profound.

We can learn from darker places, too. Steven Hassan, whose quote appears at the beginning of this chapter, is a world-renowned expert on cults. He won his knowledge painfully, by surviving an extremely controlling and abusive cult himself. Cults, or high-commitment/ high-control groups to use a less controversial term, are a fascinating, disturbing part of the human experience. It's not surprising that even this brief mention of them shows up in a section about the shadow, because it's hard to imagine a starker example of what happens when unrecognized shadow energy is let loose in the world and really gets to work. My point here reflects the observation Hassan made at the beginning of this chapter: even in the most overwhelming situations, when someone's psyche has seemingly been divorced completely from its original values, connections, and critical faculties, the core person, the "authentic self," is never really gone, even if it seems to be completely submerged in an imposed, false reality.[91] In such extreme conditions, it may take a lot of time and work to fully reconnect, but we never relinquish what makes us who we are. This understanding is my North Pole and my ultimate faith about human beings. Whether we're talking about trauma, injury, or coercion, we are never truly lost. When he describes his own experience, Hassan talks about getting flashes of thoughts or moments of doubt and disquiet, breaking through the intense mind-training he had been subjected to. Many— even most—cult members do eventually get out, and a recurring theme in the survivors' stories is that their process of leaving began not because of any dramatic event, but because one day that little voice piped up and said quietly, *Enough. It's time to go.*[92]

We may need to hear that voice many times to finally get up the strength, resources, and courage to break free, but whether we're talking about the Moonies (aka the Unification Church), the FLDS[93], an abusive relationship, or an unhealthy work environment, part of us—our unbreakable, authentic self—will tell us the truth.

Encouraging Your Intuition to Speak Up

How do you learn to hear your intuition? We'll talk about routes through the body in a bit, but you can also start by paying attention to small preferences. I practice this a lot. For example, maybe I'm walking in a park. There's one close to my house with multiple paths going around and through the trees. While I have a usual route, I try to remember to stop sometimes and get quiet. Then I wait until I feel a desire to go in one direction or another. Sometimes it's strong; sometimes it's so faint I have to wait a while to feel anything other than indifference, and even then, it's just the slightest pull. It might sound like a quick, stray thought: *that way*. My next step is to avoid justifying the answer. The whole point of this is that the indicator does not come from outside cues, like *that way is quicker to the ice cream truck*, but from some inner experience or impulse. The next thing I make sure to do is to go that way. Obeying the inner voice encourages it, and it will get your attention a bit more easily next time.

Sometimes the messages come from elsewhere, outside of our internal monitors. Maybe it takes the form of the advice you can finally, *really* hear from a friend who's been trying to get through to you. It could be a theme that seems to appear again and again in your life, from different sources: You hear a sermon, and then you see a video or read an article—maybe about a totally unrelated subject—that makes the same, unexpected point. I've had people tell me they've been confronted with the same phrase, word-for-word, by completely unconnected people, prompting them to pay attention to a particular issue. What signals or themes do you see popping up frequently?

Sometimes, we may have thoughts or even hear actual words in our head (this happens to me regularly), "come from out of nowhere." Maybe you *just know*. I've learned over the years to wake up and take notice when these messages appear in my life.

We need quiet time to see and interpret these coded signals. Distancing from the stress of your work might make you feel you are divorced from yourself, and that if you are that submerged in work, you need to build a bridge out by setting aside the space you need to reconnect. You may need a regular routine or stronger boundaries to find and defend that space. We know that self-awareness and intuition improve with practice, so making that space is worth the effort, even when it seems you have no room for any extra thing. The part of us that knows more than we think we do is waiting to talk to us. We only have to listen, and the more we listen, the more we can hear.

CHAPTER SEVEN

Pausing in the Sacred: Regulation in the Moment

"To bring to bloom the million-petaled flower
Of being here."

—Philip Larkin, *The Old Fools*

We are continuing the theme of Mourning and Remembrance here. In this chapter, we focus on the emotional work of processing stress and trauma through presence. To help us tolerate and process strong feelings, including those from past stresses and traumas, we will build on how we can be present (rather than being overwhelmed by the past or obsessing about the future) and on some in-the-moment regulating strategies to help us do that.

Deepening our capacity for regulation and presence allows us to work through things, but it also helps us think and feel at the same time, making us more effective than when we're flooded or absent. Being fully functioning at work is useful, but being fully present in our own lives is critical.

What is "the sacred" and what does it mean to pause there? Pausing in the Sacred is a phrase that psychotherapist and teacher Tara Brach uses, and I'll explain much more about it in Chapter Nine when we talk about Distraction and Flow. For now, I'll just say that in order to work with our feelings, the way we've talked about in previous chapters, we have to be able to step out of the rush of what is going on in and around us. I think "pausing" is a less intimidating word than "stopping," so we'll go ahead with Dr. Brach's turn of phrase. As for "sacred," we'll talk about religious and non-religious meanings of what it is to recognize and create the sacred, particularly in Chapter Ten about rituals. We can start creating that definition here by simply saying that our improbable existence on this fragile planet is precious and worth savoring. In the broadest sense, taking a time-out to practice regulation in the moment, to experience our existence, is to "pause in the sacred." More on that later.

I've written in *The Way Through* about several techniques for regulating ourselves in the moment. The Golden Square of attunement, attachment, attention, and adjustment is really a self-awareness and self-regulating template—both a means of recognizing where you are and the principles of getting yourself grounded again when you've become dysregulated. The CALMER Skills go further, with step-by-step instructions for working with your body, your feelings, and your thoughts. I won't reproduce them here, but I do want to talk more about finding and practicing regulation techniques, for several reasons.

First, as I tell audiences, it's important to me that you have lots of tips and tricks[94] in your back pocket. So much of our stress *about* work happens *at* work, and many of us have to plow through the day with barely enough (or no) time to do the tasks at hand, much less stop for regulation and calming. But (and this might be the heart of this book), dealing with stress in the moment, as it's happening, makes you better at your job and stops your job from harming you. This is not the same thing as gritting your teeth and barreling through a task. Your brain gets better at whatever you ask it to do a lot of. If you are asking it to freak out or shut down, it will get quicker and stronger at responding to those cues. If you ask it to learn to slow down, regain control, and regulate the body, it will get faster and stronger at doing that.

I mentioned the benefits to *you* first because I'm always trying to not-so-subtly remind you to put yourself first. But we know from the Three Empathies that being regulated also makes you better at your job helping people. That's the second reason. The third reason I included this chapter is that I know there is no one technique that works equally well for everyone, every time. I recommend trying lots of things, not just the few I wrote about in *The Way Through*, and I wanted to take the opportunity here to offer some more options. I'll talk about the principles behind these strategies that can lay the foundation for understanding, finding, and using even more techniques on your own that appeal to you.

In *The Way Through*, I explained briefly about the vagal nerve, one of the 12 cranial nerves that originate in your head and run to different parts of your body. The vagal nerve is probably key to a lot of trauma work, because it appears to work as the brakes and gas of your nervous system. This is why I always suggest to my clients and my students that they start with the body when they're trying to settle themselves down. If you're just a little agitated and nervous, some soothing self-talk might do the trick, but if you're moderately anxious or worse, all the way up to complete meltdown, cognitive strategies are likely to take a long time to make a dent.

If we start with the body, however, we can take advantage of the vagal nerve complex. The best description I have heard of this was at a trauma conference, where Deb Dana, whose work I've cited elsewhere,[95] was talking to us about helping clients get familiar with the vagal nerve. She asked the audience to imagine riding a bike down a steep hill. As you're careening down, you want to keep control of the bike, but you also want to go fast. So, you put a little pressure on the brakes, just enough to keep stable. Now imagine that you're getting close to the bottom of the hill, and you want to slow down. You gradually increase the force on the brakes—not so abruptly that you fly over the handlebars, but steadily enough to gradually slow down. She explained that in her work with clients, they would look for the body techniques that gradually engaged their vagal nerve in a controlled way, so that clients could experience what it felt like as their bike slowed down—the metaphorical equivalent of re-regulating after being hyper- or hypo-aroused.

I also talked in my book about someone telling you to "take a deep breath" when you're stressed. This is actually the opposite of what we want; the vagal nerve is engaged by slowing down the *exhale*, not by taking a big, deep *inhale*. I'll remind you here that in my experience, when a client is super-anxious, they're already aware of their breathing. They may be hyperventilating or actually panting with fear. Asking them to tune into their agitated breath seems to create an echo chamber for some people—the more they focus on their breath, the more they notice how dysregulated it is—and this seems to strengthen the message that *oh no, something terrible is happening!* That is not what we want, so I prefer to start with movement. I may ask them to do an easy Tai Chi form or yoga pose with me. This accomplishes a couple of things. First, in order to follow my very simple and slow instructions (anything complex and they'll get more overwhelmed than before), they have to stop paying so much attention to their anxiety.

There's a term for that feedback loop—*secondary anxiety*—or sometimes it's called *reactive anxiety*. It means "I'm freaking out about the fact that I'm freaking out," and much like the echo chamber we can sometimes experience with breath work, secondary anxiety just tightens the spiral. So, simple postures or movements are a nice focus for the brain, away from the experience of the anxiety. I'll give you detailed instructions in a moment, but first, I'd like to talk about Tai Chi.

I could devote this entire book and many more volumes after that to explaining Tai Chi, so I'll confine myself to this: The phrase *"tai chi"* can be translated into English multiple ways, as is often the case with the major Asian languages, and I lose nuance no matter which definition I choose. So, with apologies to Tai Chi masters and Chinese language speakers, I'll pick a couple that resonate with me. *"Tai"* can be understood to mean work or action, and *"chi,"* well, truly, this word can mean many things. Force, energy, breath, vitality—you can imagine lots of variations on this theme. My favorite description is from a Tai Chi master who guest-lectured for my class. He said that one traditional image of *chi* is "the steam that rises from a bowl of warm rice." For our purposes, let's call *chi* breath. In Tai Chi, the aim is always to use movement to connect to, and then direct, the flow of breath (energy, life force) in the body. Most of us experience that feeling as the rush of air in and out of the lungs, though masters of the art may also perceive the more subtle energy fields of the body. When you read about body-based trauma therapy, yoga is the most commonly studied and cited movement program, but Tai Chi yields similar results.[96]

Tai Chi has been linked to many health benefits, including longevity, but for now, let's explore the effect I've talked about: slowing the heart rate and the breath so we can ground ourselves in the present.

TRAILING HANDS THROUGH WATER

I am no Tai Chi instructor, but I will share the version of this form I learned. As with everything in this book, do this only if it feels OK physically and emotionally. This is a very gentle movement, and even with limited mobility, most people will not have a problem with it. Any movement or technique you use might take a moment to settle into, but nothing should feel scary or painful. For example, if you have shoulder stiffness or pain, listen to your body and lift your arms only as high as feels safe and comfortable. If it feels uncomfortable regardless of how high you're lifting, *stop doing it.* There are breath and body traditions all over the world, and if this particular technique or approach isn't for you, you can find alternatives everywhere, so don't worry about it. The principles are the same.

To begin, stand with your feet comfortably under your hips and shoulders. Your knees should feel strong and steady under you, but not locked or rigid. A slight bend or "soft knees" is fine. To feel truly balanced, you can try positioning yourself first:

Let yourself sway slowly from left to right. As you do this, notice how it feels when your weight is all the way over on one foot. Ask yourself how the bones and muscles of your feet feel with that weight (and as always, if something hurts, *stop*). We don't usually pay close attention to our feet, so don't be surprised if it takes a minute or two to get that information, and even then, the sensation will probably be subtle. Don't stress yourself about it; remember that it's the act of paying attention to being here, in your body, that we're practicing. Focus on the bottoms of your feet, your ankles, your knees, your hips, and your spine. If you aren't feeling anything, slow the movement or even stop until you notice some kind of sensation or feeling, no matter how small. Now, allow your weight to slowly shift across that foot, over the gap between your feet, and onto your other foot. If you feel wobbly doing this, find a point in the room to look at. I like to imagine the pendulum of a clock gently swinging in a straight line, back and forth, traveling the same path each time. This will also help you avoid toppling. Notice what it feels like when your weight is fully on *that* foot. Now shift back through the pendulum swing again. As you slowly sway side to side between your two feet, you'll notice more and more about how your body feels and moves as the weight shifts. When you feel like you have a sense of this information coming up from your body, slowly shorten the arc, moving less and less until you're still, with your weight evenly distributed across both feet. Now do the same thing back to front (I always start side-to-side because it's less of a balance challenge than back to front, at least for me! But you can do this in whatever order works best for you).

Staying on that center balance (right to left), let your weight slowly move from your heels through the center of your feet to the balls and toes and then back again. Now the pendulum is swaying back to front. Just as before, take your time. Let yourself get information from your body about what feels the same and what changes as the weight is redistributed. When you feel like you're tuned in to this, slowly shorten the path you're swaying on until you feel your weight evenly spread across your feet, toes to heels.

Stop and rest in that spot for a moment. You are now in a perfectly balanced place, front to back and left to right.

I find that sometimes just doing this balancing practice is enough to slow things down. But, just in case it isn't, let's add the Tai Chi form next.

Bend your elbows, keeping them lightly at your sides, and extend your forearms easily, straight in front of you. This should make a gentle 90-degree angle and should be comfortable, not stiff. Your palms are facing up. Now, tilt and lower your forearms until the backs of your hands rest on a low, invisible table, slightly below your waist, if that is comfortable. From here, gently lift your hands straight up, keeping your palms turned toward the ceiling, until they reach about shoulder height.

Without moving your arms yet, turn your hands palms-down. On the same path you went up, slowly lower your arms until your hands rest palms-down on that invisible table again. When you are at the bottom of the movement, turn your hands palms-up and lift again to your shoulder height. Your arms will always be extended to that easy, forearm-length distance away from your body throughout the exercise; you're just moving your hands up and down, along that same path, like shifting your weight back and forth on your feet when we were beginning.

That's it. That's the whole movement. While it might be more effective to stand, you can easily modify it to a sitting position if that works better for you.

Keep slowly raising your hands, palms-up, to your shoulders, turning your hands palms-down at the top, and then lowering them back down. Now, add your breath: Breathe in as you raise your hands, and then at the top, breathe out as you lower them. Keep going. As you do this, notice how your moving hands and your breath will start to sync up: If you're moving slowly, your breath will slow too. If you're breathing quickly, the movement of your hands might speed up a bit. As I was taught, this exercise is not about fixing anything. Once you have the movements down, it's not possible to do this incorrectly; however you are moving is the right way for you. The point is to check in deeply with yourself. How are you feeling today? How is your energy? Is it big and brassy, moving confidently in the air (your hands) and taking up lots of space in your body (your breath)? Or maybe it's small and subdued today, with a shorter movement up and down, and lighter breath. While other practices may work to modify what's going on, to calm or to energize you, I have found that this simple, beginner's form is powerful when you accept whatever your energy/breath/movement *feels like for you today*. Whatever it is, it's fine. Tomorrow, these things will probably feel different. That will be fine, too.

One more refinement: As you do your up-and-down, breathing in and out with each pass, maybe allow your fingers to spread apart slightly and feel the faintest resistance against them, as if you are trailing them through water. This could be the *chi* surrounding your body or simply the molecules of air around you. One teacher of mine suggested that we imagine a cloud of healing, protective golden light around our whole bodies, like the saints in medieval paintings. This life energy, she would say, flows constantly in and around our bodies, and it's always available to us, though we don't always remember to slow down enough to consciously connect with it. From a traditional Chinese view, this connecting with and moving around of the *chi* eases physical and emotional blockages, distress, and even physical illness.

Keep gently raising your hands and lowering them for as long as you like, imagining the *chi* moving in and out of your lungs and flowing around your hands the way water would swirl around them in a bath. When you are ready, take one last in-breath and go up; then one last out-breath as you come back down. Now let your hands rest palms-down on that invisible tabletop for a few seconds. Take a grounding breath in and out. This is called "letting the *chi* settle." Once the *chi* feels settled, release your hands and the practice completely. Stand there for a moment and pause. Check in with yourself and see how you feel, from your body to your emotions to your thoughts. Notice what is different and what feels the same.

Trailing Hands Through Water is just one easy example of Tai Chi, but truly, any activity that asks you to move and breathe, and notice what happens when you do is probably operating on the same principle. You can explore more Tai Chi, or yoga, or martial arts, or dance, or anything that fits you. With time and repetition, the vagal nerve will engage and slow you down, and your brain will get messages from your body that things are OK. Now, whatever positive thinking, encouraging self-talk, good old CBT, or whatever will have a much better chance of working.

Break Glass in Case of Emergency

These practices are great, but as we talked about in *The Way Through*, you have to slow down enough to recognize how stressed you are in order to use them. When we are very scared, angry, or panicking, recognition can be tricky in and of itself. I taught you the Relaxation Response in my previous book for just that reason, and now we have a deeper understanding of how and why it works. We used it mostly as a way to break into a spiral of panic or anger or shutdown so that you can use a longer technique like Trailing Hands, the CALMER skills, or some other practice. Now I want to briefly offer other strategies that may help break into that freakout spiral, so that you can ground yourself and do something more involved.

Sensory Interruption

I chose this term as a quick shorthand for a range of techniques. People who use Dialectical Behavioral Therapy, or who work with OCD, autism, or any other situation where we can get locked into a physical or emotional loop, will be familiar with sensory interruption techniques. And as is usually the case, I'm giving you a couple of easy examples; there are many versions of these, and you can try what works for you or find similar things on your own.

A quick note here: I am not including anything in this chapter that is injurious, like cutting, headbanging, biting, or what have you. This is not to stigmatize any of those practices. Like many, though not all, of my colleagues, I do see the use of those choices and do not forbid or condemn them to my clients. I point out the dangers and offer alternatives, but I offer them without judgment. My hope is that, in time, those habitual behaviors will be less attractive. My experience is that giving self-injury lots of power and mystique by banning it or ignoring its purpose by blindly criticizing counteracts my goal. This is a complicated issue, and people use these behaviors for different personal reasons. For some, self-injury probably has some of the same effects as the more benign approaches I'm describing: interrupting or replacing a distressing thought or emotion with a powerful (in this case, painful) bodily sensation. These are things that can and should be talked about in a gentle, supportive way. I am also drawing a big, bright line between nonlethal self-injury (cutting that does not involve risk of arterial bleeding, for example) to reduce emotional distress versus suicidal gestures or efforts (cutting as a trial run for an attempt). They can overlap, but not everyone who feels suicidal will harm their body in that way, and not everyone who practices self-injury is suicidal. Any suicidal thoughts, feelings, or gestures should be talked about with a caring, trained professional *immediately*.

While I don't judge self-injury, I don't endorse or encourage it either, because unlike therapeutic techniques, it can cause other problems like serious tissue damage, uncontrolled bleeding, infection, and scarring. The damage may not be merely physical, either. These behaviors may re-enact traumas or embody intense loathing and anger at the self. There is, almost always, a lot of secrecy, isolation, and shame about self-injury.

Interrupting strategies used by therapists should be completely free of those elements. If you use sensory interrupters that cause or re-enact harm, shame, or distress, you can get help and support to try new ways. But no one needs to feel bad about the urge to change how they are thinking and feeling. We start where we are.

A common example of an interrupting sensation is snapping a rubber band against your wrist. I have never pretended to be a behavior specialist, or a DBT or CBT practitioner, so I'll leave complicated explanations to them. I'll just say here that the minor (non-harmful) shock of the snap! against your wrist can be enough to interrupt the cascade of distressing thoughts or negative self-talk long enough to notice what is happening inside you and then to decide to try something else instead.

I have used variations on this with the same elements: a quick, intense but painless stimulation of one or more senses that jolts your system for a second and allows you to reset it. I heard it described once as "tripping a circuit-breaker" that stops you briefly in your tracks and then lets you change the tide of what is happening (provided you have the tools to do the next part). Ice baths are an example of a technique that can be done in a simple way: Fill a wide, shallow bowl or sink with ice cubes and very cold water. Take a deep breath and plunge your face into the water for a few seconds. I don't recommend going far enough down to submerge your ears, but that's up to you! When you need a breath, come back up, towel off, and see if you have a little more space in your thoughts and feelings to shift the direction of your self-talk. You can do the same thing with other sharp sensations: keep cut lemon wedges in the freezer and lick them (sour and cold); eat a red-hot cinnamon candy (sweet and peppery); and so on. I recently bought a couple of small plastic cylinders covered with little prickly spines for my office. The tips of the spines are blunt so they don't break the skin, of course, but also pointed enough that when you grip them tightly, they give you a neurological override of slight discomfort, which can be enough of an interruption for my clients that they can stay in their bodies and in the session.[97]

Gentler sensations can also be grounding, although they may not shock you out of where you are if you feel really locked into a spiral. I read the phrase "touching grass" as a social media-shorthand for this kind of thing: going outside and putting your bare feet on the grass, enjoying the feeling of the cool ground and tickling blades of grass on your skin as a way to interrupt distress and calm yourself down. As you'll read later, I usually try to incorporate nature into my self-care practices, and this fits nicely. Chewing on something has a similar soothing effect; the repetitive rhythm of the chewing can be regulating.

Moving into longer, more therapy-oriented techniques, you can try the Emotional Freedom Technique[98] practice that is often referred to as "tapping." A therapist who offers this technique can go into more detail with you, either in person or through one of the many online teaching videos.

I'm going to outline the tapping practice here without going into detail, just to give you a sense of what this is, and you can decide if you want to pursue more information. To practice this technique, you name your current feelings and then choose and repeat an encouraging or aspirational phrase that is the opposite of how you're currently feeling; so, "I am feeling worried and upset. Even though I feel worried and upset, I can stay calm and present," or something along those lines. You then repeat this while tapping trigger points on your wrists, head, and chest. After several repetitions through the routine, check in and see if the feelings have changed, or the affirmation should be adjusted. Often, people report feeling more regulated and present. This doesn't magically make problems disappear, of course, but it can slow the torrent of emotion enough to let you think through things differently or try to work through your situation in a new way. I have used the Emotional Freedom Technique with clients, and, like most things, I have found that it works well with some people and less so with others. It is widely recognized in the trauma and brain-body community, so you might want to check it out.

These are examples of quick, break-the-circuit interventions, as well as a few more involved techniques. Some of these, like the Relaxation Response or eating a hot candy, will be easily available to you no matter where you are, and for others, people around you won't even know you're doing it (this might be useful if they are causing your stress in the first place!). For some strategies, though, you'll need a little space and quiet. With anything involving the brain, the more frequently you practice it, the more effective it is likely to be. Most important of all, try things and see if they fit. Some of them probably will.

CHAPTER EIGHT

Refilling the Well: Regulation over Time

"Show me what you pay attention to, and I'll show you who you are."

— José Ortega y Gasset

In this chapter, we continue working with the body and the mind for our healing task of Mourning and Remembrance. Just like in Chapter Seven, we are also working on managing the present and building resilience for the future. Consistently calming and regulating ourselves over time helps us to process past things, yes, but it also may add to our ability to stay regulated during stress, and this can help insulate us from further traumatic or empathetic injury.

In Chapter Four, I mentioned that by the time the 2020 holidays came, I'd become so emotionally exhausted that I needed time to let the water in my well settle and clear, and I'll explain that more here. "The well" is my shorthand for my inner state, my own emotional presence and capacity. I've written elsewhere about my experience teaching for an amazing (truly, *amazing*) self-defense program called Impact Safety Programs. This is not a commercial for them, although I think almost anyone can benefit from what they have to teach. My point is that when I taught that class, especially the weekend-long intensive version, I was drained for days afterward. The work we did was deeply rewarding, but it meant many hours of preparation and training.

Teaching the class was time-consuming, physically demanding, and required near-constant concentration and focus from the staff. More relevantly for this book, many (though certainly not all) of our students chose to share or even rework extremely upsetting events from their lives—from emotionally abusive childhoods to rape—in some of the fight scenarios. Our job was to build and maintain a safe, nurturing space for them in which to do this; many of you know the energy and effort it takes to encourage and support such work. It was one of the great privileges of my life to be a part of this with our students, and I treasured it. But it is also true that teaching the course meant taking on a lot—physically, emotionally , and mentally—in a very short time, and I often felt both depleted and overloaded when a course ended. This was such a common experience that we talked about it often in our teaching teams, and we were careful to support one another in our post-class recovery and self-care. After doing this for a while, I started imagining that inside me was a well, one that had been used a little too much, and I learned that I had to take time to let the churning, muddy water (the emotions and stories of our students) settle. I also had to *really* rest. In a few days, it would feel like my energy and focus had returned, as if the well had filled itself up with clear, clean water again. As with everything I talk about here, this is just my personal imagery; yours might be very different. But I think it helps to have a metaphor, picture, or phrase that captures the feeling: "There's not much left in me right now, and I need to rest and replenish (energy, enthusiasm, capacity, etc.) until it comes back." So, I've titled this chapter using what resonates most for me, and you can substitute what works best for you—it's all the same thing, really. If you don't have any sense of a picture, word, or phrase for that inner state, it could be a nice exercise let yourself sit quietly for a few minutes and see what comes to mind, to discover what yours might be.

To begin, let's jump from irrigation to holidays, specifically, the New Year. I hate "New Year, new you" regimens and the idea that we human beings are like some eternal Pinterest project, always slogging away at making it look like we think it's supposed to look. So, the good news is that it's OK to decide that you are good exactly as you are. You don't have to become a morning lark if you're a night owl; you don't have to go out and buy a bunch of cute workout clothes to start moving your body more, and you don't suddenly have to become more serene than the Dalai Lama to learn a little mindfulness. The older I get, the more I recognize that the elements of my nature are just that—elemental. I'm not likely to magically transform from a nervy, anxious person to a calm, go-with-the-flow person.

However, even if we cannot change ourselves, we can grow. I think this growth can come from two starting points. First, we have to find ease in the duality of our traits. We talked earlier about Yin and Yang, opposing yet complementary, mutually dependent forces. So, I can look at the dual nature of the elements of my nature. I was avoiding the cliche "bedrock" in the past few sentences, when I was trying to define the foundational parts of ourselves, but it might be a good word to use. Let's take granite, a common "bedrock" mineral under soil and trees. Hard, unyielding, fine-grained. Are those qualities good or bad? Well, obviously, they're neither. They just are. And are we going to be able to change granite into, say, silk? Nope! So, it helps to understand the nature and qualities of granite and to figure out the contexts in which it works and those in which it doesn't. Trying to weave a filmy, lighter-than-air scarf? Silk might be nice, but don't use granite. Want smooth, durable countertops? Well, let me introduce you to granite.

As ploddingly obvious as this example is, keep it in mind the next time you get frustrated with yourself because the new self-care routine or practice you just *knew* would fix everything, didn't. Maybe it failed because you had unrealistic expectations of it: no one thing fixes every other thing. Or, and I suspect this is more likely, you had unrealistic expectations of yourself. Yes, I can drag myself out of bed for an early yoga class if it's once or twice a year. But I am a dedicated creature of the night! I struggle to make myself go to bed before midnight (OK, all right—1 a.m.). So, if I tell myself I'm going to get up at 6:30 every morning, put on my flowy, gorgeous yoga outfit that I somehow have acquired in this fantasy, and greet the day with sun salutations and a bracing cup of herbal tea, I have already failed. None of those things is going to happen. Can I get myself to stretch a little before bed, and maybe get up fifteen minutes earlier? Yep, that I can probably do. We'll talk more about setting gentle goals and then getting started on them in Chapter Thirteen, The Rhino and the Unicorn.

A great example of this was in some article I read online that talked about a common problem when it comes to organizing. We tend to find a system and try to fit ourselves into it. You buy the containers or bins or a label maker or whatever, and you usually abandon the system almost immediately, then blame yourself. The author pointed out that sometimes, trying to adopt a system that isn't natural to you is what kills the possibility of any real gain. So, he suggests looking at what you already do, and starting from there. Sure, the personalized hook plaque labeled **Keys 'N Stuff** might look great by your front door, but if you are someone who habitually slings their keys on the kitchen table when you come home after a long day, then putting them in a small basket or box *on the kitchen table* is going to be something you can actually do and will probably help you find your keys in the morning! It'll never go up to your Instagram page, but who cares?

I launched into all of this at the beginning of this chapter, because if you are like me, no longer so dewy-eyed about life and its possibilities,

I figure that, also like me, you might read a chapter title about things you have to do over time with a sinking sensation in your stomach. I usually react to these kinds of things with a mixed effect: the hopeful, optimistic part of me perks up at the idea of a whole new way of being, usually far more put-together than my life is at any given moment. But another part of me dreads yet more disappointment in myself or shrinks away from the idea of one-more-damn-thing to improve. This is not about making yourself something you are not, because there is nothing wrong with what you are now.

When I was growing up in the Midwest in the 1970s, *yoga* was such a rare word that, somewhere in my head, I confused it with yogurt (also quite exotic in my Ohio childhood) and pictured someone sitting cross-legged, holding a bowl of whitish pudding whenever it was mentioned. Now, I really don't need to tell you the benefits of yoga because they're talked about everywhere. But I can summarize what I understand about why it's being so widely embraced, from social media for fitness to the VA for trauma.[99] There are quite literally hundreds of studies about yoga, and it would be useless to try to encapsulate all of that here, but the active principles are these:

Yoga makes you pay attention to what you are doing. Whenever I mention meditation and someone says, "Oh, I could never sit still that long," I always point out two things: First, meditation is not about sitting. You can move around while you're meditating, depending on the practice, and traditions like walking meditation are thousands of years old. Second, have you heard of yoga? An instructor told me that the original purpose of yoga was not to replace meditation but to enhance it: sitting, standing, or walking for hours on end (a few of the traditional methods) required strength and flexibility, or you'd be too sore and exhausted to do the mental work of the practice. The yoga poses help build your physical condition to do the mental work while also encouraging mindful presence. Even this training, though, is an opportunity to keep paying attention. I think yoga allows us to learn about our minds along with our bodies (for example, I learned that my mind is concerned about how easily my body falls over). When I work with trauma clients, I point out that being in tension from hyper-arousal or inert from hypo-arousal is really hard on our bodies, and some gentle movement can ease the stiffness and strain of those states. So, gentle movement is the first factor. It's hard to imagine anyone, from the bed-bound to an Olympic athlete, who does not benefit from finding a way to move. But the second factor may be even more important: Yoga makes you, in the words of Ram Dass, "Be Here Now." Even in the slowest Hatha class (or as I affectionately call it, "Old Lady Yoga"), you have to pay attention to what is happening *now*. Where is your hand, now? Where are your feet supposed to be, now? What is your inhale doing, now? In terms of conscious focus, you really can't do anything else at the same time, and what a relief that can be for our tired-out, distracted brains. I think there is a third element too, if we allow it, and that is gentle observation and non-judgment.

When I talked about the CALMER skills in *The Way Through*, I focused on our judgment of ourselves—how unrelentingly pitiless and cruel we can be to ourselves, nearly every waking minute. I can only speak for my own internal experience, though I've heard many others talk about something similar. Yoga certainly offers all the comparing that the rest of life does: *Does my butt look big? Is my outfit cute enough? Hers looks like it came from that trendy store. I wonder if she thinks my outfit is tacky. [two and a half seconds here of focusing on what the teacher is saying] Wow, that guy's good at this balance pose. I can do that, too! Ha, you're not that good, Mr. I'm-So-Good-At-Balance Poses! Oh damn, I fell over. He definitely saw me fall over. Why am I so judgy and immature? [four seconds]. Does my butt look big now?*[100]

You get the idea. But what I found is that with lots and lots of compassionate reminders (remember loving-kindness?) gradually my mind was able to take longer breaks from its nonstop chatter and just notice my body and what I was asking it to do. If I had feelings of fear or insecurity, I could feel them and then let them go instead of obsessing. Little by little, my awareness became gentler. Maybe it doesn't matter if my butt looks big or my outfit isn't cool. Maybe my Secret Yoga Rival (the one who occasionally gets more attention or praise from the teacher, the one who obviously thinks they're sooo great) isn't a rival at all, has no idea we're competing, and maybe even struggles with some things I find a little easier. Maybe they're a nice person who isn't thinking bad things about me at all. In other words, yoga lets me watch my body and my experiences with a little perspective, compassion, and even humor. For those of us who struggle to find that gentleness for ourselves, and especially for trauma survivors who learned that their body is a dangerous place to be avoided, finding out how to be in your body can be nice, soothing, and even healing. That's one of the reasons why it's so popular.

Any kind of mindfulness practice helps, really. Dr. Zubin Damania, known to his fans as ZDogg, M.D. (or his beloved alter-ego, Doc Vader), is a hospitalist physician in the San Francisco Bay Area. Damania makes funny videos about medical culture, but his most serious work is about the crisis of burnout in medicine, teaching doctors, nurses, and helpers of all kinds learn to combat burnout with mindfulness practice. He talks at length on his podcasts with expert guests about many issues facing helpers, but his focus often centers on learning to consciously recognize our thoughts and feelings, so that we can have more control over our actions instead of endlessly reacting to everything.[101] He uses the metaphor of an elephant (thoughts, feelings, worries, beliefs, sensations) and a rider (our conscious awareness) *directing* that elephant rather than letting the elephant wander-or stampede-away with us. I mention his work in particular because I think many of us with advanced degrees and leadership roles, whether in therapy, medicine, psychology, or what have you, are used to assuming that our intellects are the only tool we need. Damania speaks as a peer to audiences that might otherwise have a hard time hearing that our highly educated thoughts may not always be as reliable as we think. Learning to pause and consciously observe *all* of our current experience, then choose what we really want to do, takes practice. I am always sure that I know what's going on with me just from drifting along with the constant stream of thoughts in my head, and then I sit in mindfulness practice or in a yoga pose for a few minutes, and I can suddenly see the fear, worry, distraction, or whatever has actually been droning on in there. Stopping long enough to step back and observe our thoughts stops us from mindlessly following them—like the rider gently stopping the elephant and redirecting it, rather than letting it have its own way.

Tai Chi Again, Briefly

We learned a little about Tai Chi already in regulation in the moment, and in terms of regulation over time, it is perhaps the lesser-known version of yoga, though I have seen it become more popular lately. There haven't been as many trauma studies on Tai Chi as on yoga, but I think much of yoga's healing nature can be found in the ongoing practice of Tai Chi as well. While the "forms" tend to be smaller, less strenuous movements, from my very brief experience as a beginner, the subtle elements of linking breath to movement require an even finer focus, at least for me. Adherents of Tai Chi will tell you that the movements contain power to shift and invigorate *chi*, contributing to health and longevity. Science may not have validated all these claims yet, but I will say that the idea of the energy of the body, in and around us, has a wider acceptance now than in previous years, and I suggest we stay tuned to the science in years to come. As I've said, I like using a few simple Tai Chi forms with some clients when they are struggling to experience any kind of grounding in the body. I explained one of these forms in the previous chapter, so I won't go into them here, but if any kind of exercise seems intimidating to you, or you haven't exercised in a long time, Tai Chi might feel easier to begin with than yoga as a practice to adopt over time.

RESISTANCE WORK

A similar overlap happens with other kinds of movement: We can talk about them and their usefulness in the moment, but I have made the somewhat arbitrary decision to separate them into things I think lend themselves to daily routine rather than emergency measures, and there is no better example of this than resistance work. There is no lack of studies about the benefits of resistance-based exercise for anxiety and, thus, for trauma and stress as well. Most recently, Laura Khoudari, in her book *Lifting Heavy Things*,[102] lays out a practical guide for how to approach this kind of exercise from a trauma perspective. Rather than reproduce her work here, I'll just touch on the elements that relate to how I work with trauma and stress.

First, she writes movingly about reclaiming gym space and weight training from the painful, shaming, or judgmental experiences many of us, especially (but not exclusively) women, have had at gyms, and that alone made me appreciate her work. Next, she explains that resistance (feeling something push back against you, like the floor "pushing back" when you hold yourself in a plank) engages the nervous system and gives it consistent, soothing feedback. Those of you who work with people with autism are probably very familiar with the idea of this kind of calming pressure, especially when it is self-administered and controllable by the person. When my older son was an infant, he loved to be swaddled tightly, certainly far tighter than I would like as an adult (in fact, just thinking about it now as I write this makes me feel a little panicky, but then, I tend toward claustrophobia). The wise nurse showing us how to wrap him said, "Babies are used to being very tight in the womb by the time they're ready to be born, and once they're outside of the womb, they're scared they're flying apart." I have no idea if this is true, but it's undeniable that many of us find some kind of pressure or feedback on the body's joints and limbs deeply reassuring.

I think that, like the other practices we've talked about, resistance work requires attention. With some weights, it can be incredibly dangerous not to be paying close attention to form; so dangerous, in fact, that you need a trainer or spotter with you. As we know by now, that kind of single focus can be a sigh of relief for our brains. Entering deeply into this practice, like the ones we've talked about so far, can encourage us to set down our judging self, because nobody is ever at the top of Strength Mountain. All athletes have their limits, even the gold medalist. Every lifter finds the edge of their capacity and works with that. Where that edge happens to be is irrelevant and, eventually, a bit boring. Someone will always be better than you and someone always worse, so if you can let yourself simply connect with the experience you are having, it lets you "get out from under the fatwa," as Anne Lamott would say, of our constant self-judgment."[103] Where you start and where you end up truly does not matter: We are all in the process. That is, for many of us, a profound redemption and relief from what life feels like a lot of the time.

PRAYER

This is not a religious book, and it is not my place to tell you anything about your religion or mine or anyone else's. But I do want to take as many opportunities to tell you, in as many ways as I can possibly think of, that time spent connecting to something bigger than ourselves is helpful, according to every book I've read or teacher I've ever learned from—including the teacher that is my own experience. Whether it's a gratitude practice, established worship, or simply stepping out of the profane into the sacred (see Chapter Ten), this also helps regulate and renew us over time.

YOU HAVE TO BE AROUND PEOPLE SOMETIMES (SORRY!)

In *The Myth of Normal*, Maté addresses not only what is going on *inside* of us but also what is going on *between* us. He quotes childhood trauma expert Bruce Perry, "When people start to lose a sense of meaning and become disconnected, that's where disease comes from, that's where breakdown in our health—mental, physical, social health-occurs"[104] and psychology professor Bruce Alexander about people's "vital need for social belonging with their equally vital needs for individual autonomy and achievement . . . psychosocial integration."[105]

Most of this book has addressed those internal processes, but we also need to connect with other people, *in person*. I'm not among those who think that technology has made everything worse. If you take the long view, every generation talks about how bad things are now compared to then. Hesiod was a Greek writer who complained that the past generations were strong and the current youth were weak, distracted, and soft—and he lived nearly 3,000 years ago.[106] I'm generally cheerful about the fact that things are probably never that much different from how they have ever been. But it is also true that the pandemic brought home to us how much we crave being in the same room together, being able to read the micro-shifts in someone's expression closely, or to "feel their aura" as one of your wackier friends might say. Whatever it is—energy, vibes, pheromones, or what have you—what I can tell you for sure is that once we did all come back together, at meetings and conferences, it was all anyone could talk about—how good it felt to be among other people again.

The closest I'd ever come to this sort of universal experience before COVID-19 was that very brief time in the days after 9/11. I remember stopping to talk with complete strangers at the grocery store, sharing what we'd heard, the latest conflicting, sorrowful information about how many had been lost, or what attacks might still follow. For me, the strangest, most dreamlike moment in that aftermath was in a gas station. It was near the satellite office of an agency I worked for, and it was very sketchy indeed. The people who hung around there to eat the shriveled hot dogs and buy beer were, let's say, a colorful array of tattoos, court dates, and diagnoses. Normally, I'd duck in to grab really bad coffee[107] and hustle on out again. Not on September 12, 2001. On that day, the bearded guy buying cigarettes, the gray-skinned man behind the counter (whose pallor suggested he never came out from behind the counter, and maybe didn't exist anywhere *but* behind the counter), and I all lingered to chat, asking one another, "How are you holding up?" I remember thinking at the time that this odd suspension of the rules—who talks and who doesn't, what interactions you were allowed to have and which ones would be big mistakes—was a special thing; something that would not—*could not*—last long. Of course, I was right, and it didn't. After just two or three days, we all settled back into our habitual, wary distances again. For a minute, though, we had allowed ourselves to let people know that we cared about how they were feeling. We let them care about us.

Did this little story of mine, or the callback to the end of the COVID-19 lockdown, make you feel strangely homesick for those experiences we all shared together? Then maybe that's a sign that you need more connection. If the thought of connecting to other humans makes you feel a little tense, then let me reassure you that I'm not talking about the deep, effortful interactions of work. Social scientists talk about the "soft social relationships" we have, with a neighbor we wave at, the guy who runs the corner grocery and has started to recognize and joke with you, or the lady at the laundromat who once borrowed 25 cents from you for the vending machine and now always nods hi. It turns out we humans really need our little villages, our tribes, to feel tethered to this planet. Without all that, many of us start to feel as if we're going to float away.

On the other hand, if it makes you really stressed to think about doing this, you might be too depleted. Rather than worrying about soft social interactions, it might be better to prioritize intensive healing. The connections can wait until you feel like your well has filled again.

Chapter Nine

Angels and Demons: Addiction, Distraction, and Flow

"Angels and demons can't cross over onto our plane. So, instead we get what I call half-breeds. The influence peddlers. They can only whisper in our ears. But a single word can give you courage or turn your favorite pleasure into your worst nightmare."

—John Constantine, *Constantine*[108]

I'll wrap up Mourning and Remembrance with this chapter about noticing when our brain might be taking us out of the moment and what activities may help us stay present. This extends our conversation about regulation; we'll talk about how to be immersed and engaged in ways that bring gratification and may help sustain us mentally and emotionally. For many of us, intense engagement often happens at work, which is where we also accumulate pain and stress. Learning how to experience deep involvement in other ways helps us move forward and maybe let go of the intense experiences of suffering and pain we have carried with us—not through numbness and distraction, but through deep engagement with our strengths and interests.

As a hobby, bingeing went from "very popular" to "how I just might survive this" for a lot of us in 2020. Bingeing is a laden activity for humans: usually attractive in anticipation, trance-y in practice, with lots of regret and shame afterwards. It went so far beyond food. We stopped watching TV and started bingeing it. I had to catch myself rewinding repeatedly to hear a line of dialogue because I was busy binge-shopping or doom-scrolling (binge-worrying?) on my phone, to distract myself during my *other* distraction.

I'm far from an expert in eating disorders, but I'm interested in bingeing. We start out wanting to feed ourselves, either with actual food, or with other things—information, stories, whatever. But by definition, bingeing means going past *what-we-need* to *too-much*. With eating, your body only needs so much food, and once you've eaten past that point, you can't really nourish yourself anymore, because you now have more than your body can use. You have to vomit, purge, or just lie around uncomfortably until you can slowly process the excess that you just took in. There are lots of specifics about the experience of bingeing, and this is not a clinical chapter but an emotional one, so I'll touch on just a few of these. I started the chapter with the most important stages: anticipation or craving, trance, and then shame. Just typing those words brings up feelings and sensations for me, and maybe for you, too.

CRAVING

The anticipation and craving for a binge are signals that I'm stressed or uncomfortable, and the pandemic was an endless buffet of stress and discomfort. It reminded me of the months after my mother died. I was running back and forth across the state to help my siblings deal with her house and her affairs, then driving back to work a demanding full-time job, with a husband and two small children at home. To say this created "discomfort" is not quite right: "Horrible pain, anger, sadness, exhaustion, and disorientation" would be closer to it. Those first months have a lot of haze around them in my memory, but I do remember my rare times at home being completely taken over by reading. I went from being an early, devoted reader to an addict. This may sound like I'm being adorable—and I'll grant you that as addictions go, reading isn't as instantly destructive as, say, methamphetamines—but trust me when I tell you there was nothing adorable about it for the people around me. Reading took me out of my painful thoughts and my confusing emotions. I was stashing books in odd places around the house, the way alcoholics hide bottles, snatching moments to read when I could have been connecting with my husband or doing some parenting. All of these books were well-read and familiar to me already, so it's not like I was learning or doing something necessary for work. This isn't recrimination or self-denial; it's just true.

For months, I checked out as a parent and as a partner. When my sons wanted my attention or my husband gently tried to engage me to participate when I was off reading somewhere, I could be irritable and resentful—and on a couple of occasions, red-faced and shouty. As soon as I could plausibly get away, I'd head off to read some more. This was years before smartphones. Had it happened today, I know for sure that books would have been replaced by my phone, glued to my hand while I compulsively played "one more" game or endlessly refreshed "one more" political blog. The phone would have been my new escape hatch. It doesn't matter—it's all the same thing. Back then, from some cool corner of my brain, I watched myself doing this obsessive reading, and even in my blurry pain, it was clear, absolutely, that what I was doing was not OK. Reading to the point of consistently absenting myself from my family and my obligations was not OK. *I* was not OK at all. So, in the spring of 2020, watching half a season of *Mad Men* in one sitting, just to finish it off and start the next one tomorrow, was sneakily familiar. Like that time almost 20 years earlier, though, it was much easier to observe myself doing it than it was to stop. And stopping is the problem, isn't it?

TRANCE

There have been literal volumes written about the effects of compul-sive, repetitive behavior on the brain, from hitting those dopami-nergic circuits for reward to dulling awareness and shutting off satiety. I'll sum it up here with the word *away*. Among the Irish, when you momentarily check out, with inspiration (if you're a poet) or internal stimuli (if you're schizophrenic), they say that you're "away with the fairies." Who could come up with a more beautiful way to say how badly we humans sometimes need to be anywhere but here? Here is hard. Here, sometimes, is excruciating, beyond horrible. I certainly can't deny the allure of Away.

Of course in the old stories, when people finally do return from their time among the fairies, they find that a hundred years have passed, or the gold they were given as payment has been transmuted to straw and dung. In other words, we lose time out of our lives and come back from Away with nothing to show for it. In some versions of the story, the person who comes back from the fairies dies within days of returning home. I think these folk images are typically coded, world-soul language for this truth: Habitually trancing out doesn't really give you anything in the long run; it only takes. Spend too much time Away and you return empty-handed, with nothing waiting for you.

This wisdom leads us nicely to the last part of the binge: regret.

REGRET

"Lots of regret and shame—that should be the
slogan for Snakejuice."
—Ann Perkins, *Parks and Recreation*

Shame is hard to untangle because it's so personal and specific to each of us. Let's say that the nature of bingeing leads each of us to what we don't want, whether it's too much food, wasted time, or spending more money than we planned. Studies find that there's an optimal point in TV watching, when we have felt the most relaxation and enjoyment we're going to get from it, and then after that, it drops away sharply. Like too much food, too much TV leaves people feeling sad, tired, and listless. Too much shopping can be even more vicious, leading to years of pain and distress after the event if it takes you down into debt, worry, and fights.

When is it addiction?

There is a whole profession dedicated to recognizing, supporting, and treating addiction. As a therapist who works with trauma, I consider myself to be addiction-conversant but certainly no expert. If you're worried, the best advice I can give you is to talk with someone who *is* an expert, at a clinic where addiction is treated, or with a counselor who specializes in this. What I can do is give you a sense of how addiction is diagnosed and encourage you that there are a whole lot of wise, compassionate people who have devoted their lives to understanding and supporting those of us who grapple with this.

In the DSM-5, the substances that people might overuse or misuse include:

- alcohol
- caffeine
- cannabis (THC)
- hallucinogens (for example, LSD, mushrooms)
- hypnotics or anxiolytics ("benzos")
- inhalants (aerosols, nitrous, etc.)
- opioids (pain meds; heroin)
- sedatives
- stimulants (cocaine, meth)
- tobacco

The DSM also includes one behavioral category: gambling. As of this writing, no other behaviors such as eating, shopping, or sex are considered formally as addictions or diagnosable disorders, though the brain chemistry of reward, habituation, and medication very well may be involved in those, too, and our lists will almost certainly change in the years to come.[109]

Other criteria include things like habituation (increased tolerance); craving; risk-taking; and damaging our personal, professional, or social lives due to dependence on or overuse of a substance.

Now, like everything else in this book, this section is meant to give you some information to start with, and gently suggest you look further if this resonates for you. It is not a do-it-yourself substance abuse assessment kit. Also, I'm going to *beg* you not to get a diagnosis for yourself or anyone else from Dr. TikTok, PhD. I do, however, want to talk a little more about the relationship between substance use/misuse/addiction and pain.

For this, we will return to our friend, Dr. Gabor Maté. I won't try to reproduce whole chapters of *The Myth of Normal* here, but I will share a few points from his deep understanding of these miseries. We'll start with this one: "Ask not why the addiction, but why the pain."[110] He is saying that from a trauma-informed perspective, substance abuse and addiction can be considered symptoms rather than the core issue. We are driven to relief when we are in too much pain, too often, for too long. People who don't experience that much pain are, in his view, less likely to seek and then become dependent on pain relief in the first place.

Remember those famous rat experiments where the rat chooses cocaine over food and water and eventually dies? Those experiments left out a pretty important part of the story. Rats, incredibly smart and social animals that they are, were kept isolated in bare cages in a sterile laboratory setting. No wonder they compulsively hit the bar to get the cocaine solution. When researchers recreated those experiments recently, they put some of the rats in lush, comfortable environments, with other rats to bond with and lots of toys and puzzles to engage them, or as one researcher put it, Rat Paradise. And guess what? Those rats were not likely to choose the cocaine.[111] The terrified, lonely, bored rats were. In other words, our levels of pain, stress, and isolation *matter* when it comes to the risk of addiction.

I should say here that Dr. Maté does not speak for the entire field of addiction, nor do I think he would claim that he does. There are certainly professionals who disagree with his views, but I think it is widely accepted among substance abuse specialists that trauma and emotional pain at least play a role in many people's stories of addiction. His argument that "only a person in pain craves anesthesia" may not account for every single instance of substance dependence, but I think it does reflect an emotional truth that we return to again and again in this book—if we find ourselves consistently craving escape, maybe we'd better look at what it is we need to escape from, and try to change *that,* rather than finding ever-more powerful and seductive ways to not be present.

Here's more of what Maté has to say:

> Addiction is a complex psychological, emotional, physiological, neurobiological social and spiritual process. It manifests through any behavior in which a person finds negative consequences, and yet the person refuses or is unable to give it up. Accordingly, the three main hallmarks of addiction are: short-term relief or pleasure and therefore craving; long-term suffering for oneself or others; and an inability to stop.[112]

I often shy away from discussing substance abuse when I talk with audiences about "anesthesia" in our coping strategies, because I don't have space with them to process this more carefully, with each individual. But this is what I would encourage you to consider for yourself. As Maté says, "While more precise and more hopeful, my definition . . . makes addiction's "big tent" even bigger. You might just find yourself under it."

What Is Distraction Doing to Us?

In the past few years, I've seen variations on the same headline. "You're Not Losing Your Memory—You're Distracted."[113] The point runs in two directions: Don't worry about your cognitive change just yet, because there might be an easy(ish) fix, and also, your cognition is getting worse. The message is consistently pointing to constant distraction as the cause, and for most of us, it's our phones. We have power literally in the palms of our hands that past generations would have had to sell their souls to glimpse. "Faustphones" should have been what Steve Jobs called his neat little products. And I'll spare you the sermons about the dangers of being constantly on our phones since you probably know them already. But if you're fretting about decreased ability to focus, to enjoy what you're doing or to remember why you came into the room, try putting your phone down consistently before you call your doctor. Of course, there can be other factors (hi, menopause), and we'll talk about stress much more in a later chapter.

Stress is no doubt both driving us to, and feeding on, our obsession with our phones. Rather than yet another scolding, I'd like to point out what is fascinating about our brains' attention and why we might cherish it. Valuing something new is a nice way to back away from something unhealthy rather than being endlessly lectured about how bad it is.

So, here is how amazing your brain really is. You'll need a partner to do this to really experience the effect. Ask them to Google (probably on their phone! I know) the term "inattentional blindness" and find an older-looking video that is set in a gym. Have them make sure to cover up anything that might tip you off in the title or the comments, and then watch it. Come back after that.

Did you watch the video? If you didn't, but you'd like to check it out later,

STOP.

READ NO FURTHER.

SKIP TO THE NEXT SECTION.

OK, if you're still here then either you watched the video, or you just don't care that much about brain science and/or narrative whimsy in books. All good either way, so let's get into it.

Did you see the gorilla? I didn't, like the majority of the people who watched that video.[114] This experiment, first conducted by Arien Mack and Irvin Rock in 1988 at the University of California, Berkeley, gave us the term "inattentional blindness." When we are focused on one thing, we really do become largely blind to even the most astonishingly obvious things happening around us. And *blindness* is perhaps a deceptive term because this is a brain issue, not an eye issue. In fact, the really crazy thing about "the gorilla experiment" is that in motion sensor tests, the eyes of the people who didn't notice the gorilla spent about as much time resting on it as the eyes of people who did see it. Your eyes didn't miss it, in other words. Your brain did. What we are looking at *and registering in our conscious awareness* is called the "zone of fixation."[115]

While all of this is partly to give you a fun activity in the middle of this book, I do have a couple of thoughts. First, if your zone of attention is your phone, imagine how many wonderful, rewarding, dangerous, or powerful things are escaping your notice, constantly. Humans have always struggled not be preoccupied with our thoughts and worries and just Be Here Now, but phones are literally more stimuli than our brains have evolved to handle. No wonder we keep using the word "addiction." Like heroin, it might just be too powerful, more than most people can do to tear themselves away easily. Second, what exactly *is* it that's holding your attention on that thing? There are quite literally millions of answers to that question, anywhere at any moment on earth, but my guess is that a distressing number of us are, at any given moment, looking at something that makes us feel ugly, unloved, poor, and of no consequence. Sappers of contentment and thieves of self-acceptance. You might know these things by their more familiar name: Advertisements. Sometimes we do actually need to buy things, but often, at least for me, I find myself pulled far beyond that to things that I've been convinced I want, but don't really need.

Advertisements are so rooted in our culture that they have become, like the gorilla in the gym, completely invisible to us, but they're there, feeding on our boredom and sorrow. The core mechanism of advertisements is simple and, when you think about it, quietly cruel. Here is how many of them are designed: *We'll point out a "problem" you have. It might be a problem that all human beings have, like feeling lonely sometimes. It might be a problem that cannot be fixed or, alternatively, doesn't really need to be fixed. If you don't have a problem at all, then we'll make you* think *you have a problem* (youngsters reading this, Google "dishpan hands"). *Now we'll tell you what you can do to solve this problem, and guess what? It costs you only money. The more ads you see, the more money you'll find you need to have, so the more you're going to have to chase money. And you will never run out of problems because we'll never run out of things to sell, so you can spend all that money you just gathered, and then go get more, and so on, forever.*

Advertisements create longing, which exists only when we lack something. So, we must always be lacking. No wonder nothing, and no one, is ever "enough." Some of us wear bracelets or T-shirts or even *get tattoos on our skin* to try to remind ourselves that this message of fundamental lacking is a lie.[116] What a strange arrangement! I've watched the creep of this artificial longing being jammed into every conceivable space. There are ads playing while we are shopping, *spending money on things we already saw in other ads.* There are ads all over "social" media. And social media, make no mistake, is often just more ads; either explicitly for products, or even more insidiously, the ads we are running for other people about ourselves. If our attention creates our reality so powerfully, then making choices about our attention is really making choices about the reality in which we want to live.

We can reclaim our attention, which is to say, we can reclaim our reality. A current trend is "monotasking,"[117] which can include things like reading, sleeping, learning, and a really mind-blowing one, eating. Seriously, when was the last time you ate anything bigger than a snack with *nothing but the food to occupy your attention?* Truthfully, it makes me uncomfortable just thinking about that, which means I probably need more practice doing it. With respect to this version, it's really the wisdom of the ancients, repackaged: Mindfulness. Slowness. Intention. There are 12 things in the monotasking book, but I think all of human life can be given the honor of our full attention. That honor is described beautifully by Tara Brach, who earlier in this book gave us the Wings of the Bird exercise for working with emotion. She describes the sacred as "having dedicated myself to what I call pausing and deepening attention within myself . . . what I call the 'sacred,' where I would, before I'd say anything, I would get more intimate with my own experience. I was coming from a place of more balance, more equanimity. But I was also inquiring more about [the experience of others]."[118]

Brach talks about the need for time and space to think and process, even (maybe *especially*) when that space contains uncomfortable feelings, rather than numbness and distraction. She calls this space the "pausing in the sacred." In the next chapter, I'll talk more about what makes something "sacred," but I'll just touch on it here briefly. "Sacred" here doesn't mean religious, but I think Brach would say that setting time and space apart to really think and feel, even when it's just for a moment or two, connects us to something bigger and more important than the constant flow of sensation and distraction we spend so much of our time swimming around in. More important than just reclaiming our time and awareness, we can also find healing. What Brach describes in this pause is the chance to deepen our experience, to see what's under our boredom, or our anger, or our anxiety. She is talking about the important discomfort we have to *learn to be with* rather than instantly banish, hungry for the next soothing distraction. As I wrote in the last chapters, we're also missing that moment to choose which thoughts are reliable and which are not, which feelings need to be acted upon and which ones we should sit with for a while first. Existentialist therapist Rollo May talked about this long before cell phones—what we lose when we no longer have that moment to ourselves: "Human freedom involves our capacity to pause between stimulus and response and, in that pause, to choose the one response toward which we wish to throw our weight."[119] If we use that sacred pause, we connect not only to our experience, but we also get a little foothold on how we want to interact with the person in front of us. So now, we're affecting their reality too. What could be more important than this chance to stop and reflect, to be conscious and present, rather than reflexive and unconscious of what we're *really* doing? Whatever that might be, it probably doesn't come in the form of distraction.

Angels and Demons

Bingeing is how nourishment, enrichment, and pleasure become drivenness, self-removal, and regret. I think the description the character Constantine gives us is pretty apt. Now let's turn our gaze away from the demons and toward the angels.

FLOW

"I believe that God made me for a purpose . . . but He also
made me fast. And when I run, I feel His pleasure."
—Eric Liddel, Olympic runner, *Chariots of Fire*[120]

Decades ago, Mihaly Csikszentmihalyi and Jeanne Nakamura identified and made popular the lovely concept of Flow: "Optimal experience is thus something we make happen . . . For each person, there are thousands of opportunities, challenges to expand ourselves."[121]

You may recognize it from interviews with athletes about "being in the zone." We call it cooking with gas, hitting on all cylinders, jamming. Intuitively, we usually describe the sensation of moving at great speed rather than the no-place stuckness of Away or of trance and binge. Flow has been a central pillar of positive psychology since the 1970s, so you've probably heard of it, but I'll give you a list of some of its most recognizable elements.

Clear Goals

A Flow experience has clear, attainable goals. If you're baking sourdough (a little callback here to the shared delusion of 2020 when, as a species, we all agreed to pretend that sourdough is not The Worst Of The Breads), you know when you're done because now you have a loaf of (ugh) sourdough, and before, you didn't. Goal attained. When many of us are lucky enough to experience moments of Flow at work (more on that in a minute), much of the time, there is not an obvious goal or endpoint to what we're doing. Lifelong support for an individual if you're staff, constant wrangling for money and resources if you're a director, the eternal struggle to hire and keep quality staff— we have victories, but we're never done, and the work stretches out in front of us endlessly. When you take a step back, the "work" of helpers began long before we were born and will continue long after our little lives are over. So, a clear, attainable goal can be innately soothing and attractive to us.

Immediate Feedback

Close on the heels of that attainable goal is the feedback on how we're doing. As a therapist, I sometimes have Flow moments when it seems my words and actions produce clear insights in the person sitting across from me, but that's not always how it happens. Often, therapy is a slow process, and much of the action happens offstage in the small decisions and gradual changes a client notices in themselves over time.

By way of contrast, if you're making your way up a climbing wall at a gym, you either catch that toehold or you slip down. You know right away whether you've succeeded or not, and you can see an almost immediate impact of your action at any moment.

Merged Actions and Awareness

For me, merged actions and awareness feel distinct from feedback, although I'm not sure I can explain just how. Maybe it's that what you do is in an almost-continuous loop. When I'm talking in front of a class or an audience, I sometimes feel like my awareness of what I'm saying, the choice to go in a different direction, the feedback from the audience about whether they're with me or not, and then the next moment of decision about the next words, all braid together in a ribbon coming out of my mouth, without any noticeable seconds' gap to think consciously about it. That's what it feels like to me when actions and awareness merge.

Complete Concentration

This one speaks for itself. You really can't bake *and* scroll on your phone *and* answer your kid's question all at the same time. Most of the actions of baking, like measuring, slicing, checking for doneness, or decorating, require you to pay full, close attention to what you are doing.

Un-self-consciousness

I think one of the most glorious parts of Flow is the loss of the inner critic. When things are going well for me onstage, I can forget, for a blessed few minutes, my ongoing internal yammer. I don't know about you, but I never miss that voice when it takes a break, and I can be truly present to what is happening.

Sense of Control

Flow allows us to be in at least some control of what is happening. *We* are the one speaking, cooking, creating, climbing. We are in charge of our experience and, to some extent at least, our results.

Challenge and Skill

Unlike passively zoning out in front of the TV, Flow activities demand a lot from us. They are hard. They require effort, like scaling a wall. They require concentration, like carefully measuring ingredients. They require acts of imagination, emotional honesty, and intuition when creating art. Many of these activities also mean gathering prized materials (making that heirloom quilt) or gaining a time-consuming skill. As any artist or creator will tell you, building facility and skill is a pursuit that never ends; there's always more to learn. When an activity becomes easy and repetitive, it probably no longer offers Flow.

Transformation of Time

I've heard elite athletes talk about time slowing down when they are in their zone, their Flow. Either of the great Ms. Williamses might tell you that when she's in that state, it seems like she has all the time in the world to leisurely make her way over to that tennis ball and hit it squarely—even though all we in the audience see is a blur as she sprints across the court and swings the racket almost too fast to see. Unlike the numb suspension of time in Away, Flow time passes quickly ("Wow, I've been painting for hours!"), but we feel the impact of it when we're done, rather than a blank. We may be sore or tired, but we can remember every minute of what we've been doing.

Intrinsic Rewards

Flow has a clear goal and often leaves a tangible product at the end— you have a planted garden bed or a new painting to show for your efforts. But Flow also gives us a deep sense of satisfaction and reward for its own sake. Long after the flowers have gone to seed or the cake has been eaten, we feel proud and accomplished for what we've done.

Character Strengths

This is distinct from skill, though they have a relationship with each other. Our character strengths play their own role in positive psychology, and much of the initial research into them was done through The Happiness Project at the University of Pennsylvania, then developed into the Values In Action (VIA) survey.[122] We know that Flow tends to occur when we're accessing those strengths—inborn traits of appreciation, intuition, creativity, or tenacity. Like Eric Liddel running in the hills of Scotland, we feel God's pleasure when we use our gifts.

And finally, the effect I've hinted at in all these examples:

Gratification

Gratification is something separate from pleasure. Pleasure, in positive psychology, is usually quick and sensory-based. It's also fleeting, and we tend to habituate to it quickly. That first spoonful of delicious ice cream registers strongly and releases dopamine. We can get a little more out of it if we go slowly and work on savoring—really noticing the details of cold, creamy, sweet, or chocolatey. But after a few more spoonsful (usually about three, according to some estimates), we habituate to it, and our brain stops registering the sensations so strongly. Flavor and texture become familiar, and the pleasure decreases fast. It's an effect called *sensory-specific satiety*, and various studies over the past decades have explored why our brains habituate so quickly and lose the sensation of pleasure. A more recent study suggested that this effect may be even more common for us now, since highly processed, attractive foods are so widely available.[123] This is why finishing a bowl of ice cream can somehow go from feeling like a treat to a chore as we plow through the rest of it. And this, of course, is the perfect runway to a binge—we try to recapture the pleasure with more, more, more—but with diminishing returns.

There's a whole area of study about slowing down, savoring, and deepening sensory enjoyment—mindful eating is just one example of this kind of practice. This also contributes to psychological positivity. Maté talks about the contrast between pleasure and gratification. Pleasure, he says, starts a flood of dopamine in the brain. This is a fast, powerful reward and is, in his opinion, the neurochemical basis of all forms of addiction. But gratification is a different animal. Gratification (Maté calls this *satisfaction*, but these terms seem to be mostly interchangeable depending on who you read) is related to serotonin release. It takes longer to release serotonin in the brain, it often requires more effort, and serotonin affects us more slowly.

According to Maté, serotonin is never associated with addiction.[124] Gratification comes after effort, concentration, skill, flexibility, responding to feedback, and achieving a hard goal. In other words, it's born directly from Flow. I sometimes picture a rock climber at the top of some crazily steep cliff she's just crawled up, inch by sweaty, scary inch (by the way, this climber does not look anything like me, even in *my* imagination. In this scene we've created, I can be found loitering around at the bottom of the cliff, eating all the snacks we packed, and congratulating myself on my good sense). So how does the climber feel? Tired, probably, with aching shoulders, scraped, stinging knees, and cramped fingers—and elated. That is gratification.

It tends to go deeper, last longer, and impact our positive view of ourselves in a much more transforming way than pleasure. Bonding with people helps release oxytocin and vasopressin; cardio from running on a treadmill (or *scampering* up that cliff, I guess) can release endorphins, which suppress pain; practicing yoga (more on that in a minute) helps our brain receive waves of soothing GABA, which helps us to relax. We humans need all of these neurological experiences, not just quick hits of rewards.[125]

> Saint Anthony said, in his solitude, he sometimes encountered devils who looked like angels, and other times he found angels who looked like devils. When asked how he could tell the difference, the saint said that you can only tell which is which by the way you feel after the creature has left your company.
> —Elizabeth Gilbert, *Eat, Pray, Love*

When I talk with audiences and students about Flow, I usually end with this quote. Gilbert is drawing from a probably apocryphal story from the Early Christian figure Saint Anthony. A monastic, Anthony spent the proverbial years alone in the desert. The idea that angels and demons can be hard to distinguish has always resonated with me, and if you are of a spiritual bent, you may have heard this—that some malevolent entities' favorite disguise is that of shining light and beauty. Certainly, it's the perfect metaphor for bingeing and Flow. One looks easy and attractive, luring us with quick sensory pleasure and enjoyment, but mostly offers us the relief of Away. Flow usually asks the opposite. We have to try hard, concentrate fiercely, and sometimes sacrifice a lot of comfort, but in exchange, we win lasting gratification and accomplishment.

The truth is that this metaphor falls apart a little in the face of human nature. The truth is that we need both: escape and presence, checking out and focusing in. Maybe the gentler term for bingeing is *anesthesia*, and I usually use this word with my clients. A little ice cream (preferably eaten straight from the container, while standing in front of the freezer), a quick social media dopamine hit, or maybe some frivolous thing on Etsy that's just what you didn't know you always needed—who could deny you a little relief from your pain? Certainly not me. And when a client is grieving or healing from deep wounds, I try to help them find the space and latitude to do just this—to let themselves have these small moments of pleasure. But we also talk about the angels and demons, that shift when the momentary pleasures turn into *more, more, more*—and then finally become too much. And that's when we may shift from dopamine to serotonin and look for moments of satisfaction instead.

I think most of us have some sense of this, although speaking for myself, learning the line of too much has been retroactive; for years, I could see it only in the rearview mirror after I went speeding past it. Age and experience have made it a little easier to see Away coming up ahead of me. It doesn't always work, but sometimes now I can slow down and then stop. My clients and I try to find that discernment and then make those choices. It takes time and practice, with a lot of errors. My favorite part of Gilbert's take on this story speaks directly to this: In the moment, a demon and an angel can look a lot alike. It's only when they leave that we know what has been with us. Sitting in the aftermath, observing our feelings, helps us learn which is which. So, if you're asking yourself about your own balance, "When is it a little anesthesia, and when is it too much? When is it nourishment and when is it binge?", it can help to notice how you feel afterwards. Do you feel fed and replenished, or sluggish? Are you pleasantly tired and relaxed, or dazed and numb? These are such interior experiences that we usually have to answer these questions alone (unless the anesthesia and binges have been literally damaging, and now we're dealing with addiction and destruction. Those usually become visible to others).

A last paraphrase from Elizabeth Gilbert: Angels leave us feeling lighter, better, stronger, encouraged, and helped. Demons leave us feeling depleted and alone.[126]

PART THREE

Reconnecting and Integrating

We move now to Herman's final task of healing from trauma: Reconnecting and Integrating with the world. In some trauma healing, there is a particular group or community that will help with this, like support groups for survivors, veterans' groups, or other circles of people who've been where you are. It also means connecting with the world as a whole. We'll start in this chapter with the connection we feel to our deep self and the world through rituals, and we'll finish with chapters Twelve and Thirteen.

CHAPTER TEN

Doorsteps, Circles, and Baths with Trees: Daily Rituals

"Between every two pines is a door leading to a new way of life."

—*John Muir*[127]

Humans communicate constantly. The complaint I hear the most in my office is how overwhelmed my clients feel, and there are a lot of reasons for this, ranging from terrible trauma to the boring struggles of ordinary life. But we're also overwhelmed by the cognitive effort of taking in written and spoken communication. We are never *not* looking at our phone to scroll through all of human knowledge, aka the Internet (reading), or sending a text (writing), going through to a voicemail or catching a podcast (listening), or leaving a message for someone (talking). It does not seem to end, ever. We are talked out. We can't read or write or listen to one more thing.[128]

I think this is why, when I'm giving a speech or a lecture, even the shortest exercise in quiet, bare attention or mindfulness usually brings my audience members a sense of relief. When you pursue them further, mindful awareness (or groundless meditation) and goal-directed (grounded) meditation can be agonizingly hard work, but initially, we usually find any sort of meditation restful and restorative, if only because we get a few minutes of peace—a tiny reprieve when we're not taking in or sending out anything to the world, resting in Brach's sacred pause.

I've written in the previous chapter about what the hidden meaning of "binge-watching" might be. This points us to a deeper human need, I think, and that is the hunger for deep images. Without diving all the way to the bottom of the anthropology pool, I'll just say that long before human beings could vocalize a complex language, and certainly before written words, we probably communicated among ourselves with the images of enacted stories, which became rituals. Universal literacy, a world in which everyone can read and write a few common languages, came along about maybe five minutes ago in the timeline of human history. In fact, for most of our time as recognizably human creatures, we communicated with simple images, sounds, movement, and dances. We went to sacred places and did sacred things.

And what makes a place, or a dance, or a picture sacred to us? Staying out of the question of the Divine, what makes humans view something as sacred is usually our behavior around it. This includes keeping something set apart, rarely used, or hidden from the view of others. Certainly, it is meant only for a single purpose. In my grad school days, I learned the definition (possibly outdated by now but useful for our purposes here) that a sacred ritual is the enactment of a myth. In other words, the myth (story) gets acted out in song, dance, or pictures, again and again. The story might be the sacrificial death of a god, or the return of spring, or the creation of the cosmos. When you do the same acting-out of the same story, in the same place, at the same time, in the same way, you imbue that action with great power. Ritual could also be called "consecrated action."[129] The repeated behavior is powerful, significant, or holy because we decide it is. This is probably the oldest way we learned to experience and share important things. I think TV and movies reflect that craving for those deep stories, powerful images, and transformative experience—and maybe we demand more and more amusement because we can barely subsist on it, trying to fill up on largely empty fluff, rather than the rich meat that used to feed us.

And I mention all this in a book about burnout and self-care because when we are in dire need of rest and healing, I think we can go back to some of our earliest human impulses. When we need to *feel* in our bones and our heart, we use ritual to help us do that. Obviously, it's a very short jump from rituals to religion, and I am not talking about that here. If you have a religious tradition that is meaningful and positive for you, this material will fit right in. If not, ritual with a small "r" will do just fine. But when we are in distress and in great need, rituals help send those messages deep down into our psyches. Here are some common examples of types of rituals:

- Liminal
- Cleansing
- Transcendent
- Communion

At the end of this chapter, I'll list some simple ideas that may be a foundation for a routine of your own, or even just to confirm that a half-conscious routine you already have may be more important than you thought. There will be more prompts at the end of this book.

LIMINAL: STEPPING OVER THE THRESHOLD

Let's start with liminal. I've always loved this word, because in its simplest form, it means doorway or threshold—a *limen*. But I also associate it with a greater sense of *passing between two worlds*, and in comparative studies and anthropology, it often has that connotation. In case this is all starting to sound too academic for words, don't worry; it has down-to-earth implications for us here.

My favorite example of liminality comes from one of the most warm, familiar figures in our modern-day gallery of archetypes: Mister Rogers. It may seem odd, when you think about it, that each episode involved a slow progression of taking off a jacket, taking off shoes, putting on other shoes, and then yet another wardrobe change into a woolly cardigan—only to reverse it all at the end. I don't remember any explicit reason in the show for him to do this (like a TV host changing into a painting smock before an art segment). It's sweet, doddering, and slightly puzzling to us adults, all this methodical fussing around with clothes, but any anthropologist could tell you what he was really up to. Mister Rogers was telling us a story about moving between worlds—and our very young brains understood that story, even though we weren't consciously aware of it. My guess is that from his incredibly intuitive and well-informed understanding of young children, he knew that any repetitive act is soothing, but he also understood that children need a signal that "something is starting" and "something is ending." As an ordained Presbyterian minister, he was probably quite conscious of the long religious pedigree of rituals and how they work on the human psyche.[130] When we watch him and vicariously join him in taking off a jacket (outside clothes), putting on a sweater (inside clothes), etc., we are moving from the entire external world (a.k.a. real life) to the internal world he has created for us (a.k.a. Mister Rogers's house). There are occasional segments out in the Neighborhood, but we're still in this created place in TV Land that we entered with him at the beginning of the episode. The show will proceed, and then when it is over, the inside clothes will be exchanged for outside clothes again, and we will leave with Mister Rogers and go back out into the world and the lives that we know. The opening and closing credits of the show both feature a shot of his front door: it doesn't get much more liminal than that!

Another obviously liminal moment is when the trolley took us (through the viewer's eye of the camera) into a tunnel, emerging into the Kingdom of Make-Believe, a life-sized, entirely separate world of imagination. If you think back or watch old videos now, you'll notice that season after season, they never varied these ritualized transitions in the show; never jazzed things up with new graphics or musical cues, never had the trolley emerge somewhere else, never even gave Mister Rogers a different place to hang his jacket. Always the same, every time. Repetition imbues power.

Interesting, but why are you telling me this? You ask. Well! Remember, during the pandemic, all the articles talked about the stress of working from home? One theme that came up time and again was "I never leave work." If you were one of the people working from home, you probably knew, consciously, that your work was finished or your meetings were done for the day, but it didn't feel like it. Never being done with work is physically and mentally exhausting. I've talked elsewhere in this book about our perpetual plugged-in-ness and the toll it takes, but this was that problem taken to an extreme.

No one can work all the time, always on the clock, never resting, never free. But many of us felt that, at least psychologically, that's where we were. I remember a popular meme joking about the odd sameness of every day; one version referred to "Today's date, Blursday the fortyteenth of Maprilay." As we've said in the *Graffiti* chapter, these jokes reflected deeper feelings, and for many of us, they helped pinpoint and express our unease about the strange, *every-day-blends-into-the-next* limbo we found ourselves in. That melting sameness was probably due, at least in part, to the loss of our liminal routines and rituals that bounded the segments of our time.

A liminal ritual can signal to the oldest part of our consciousness—the one that responds to symbols and story even under our full awareness—that something important has happened or changed. So, when you create a routine that incorporates meaningful imagery for yourself, it's a way of building a doorway in your mind. I worked with a law enforcement officer, and she talked about how she left her "work world" behind. This was vital to her for two reasons. On the one hand, she needed a deep signal to herself that she was done and could rest and restore herself after a hard day of work. On the other, she also needed to feel she was protecting her family from the sometimes-ugly world she had been submerged in all day. Some days were boring, paperwork-filled slogs, but others involved violence, anger, fear, and horror. When she went home, she wanted to feel that she had left all that behind and was not bringing any of that (emotional, spiritual, or whatever word you like) contamination home to her family. So, her daily habit was to come into the house, say a brief hello, and immediately head up to shower and change into comfortable clothes. There are multiple layers of practicality here, of course—certainly for most of us, sweatpants and a soft T-shirt help us wind down better than the heavy uniform or constricting work clothes we've worn all day. But for her, the ritual also marked a doorway that she would walk through, to leave one world and all the suffering it contained behind her so she could enter a different, safe, and serene one. We'll talk more in a moment about the profound symbolic meaning of the water in her shower, but for now, it's the transition we're focusing on.

Finding a way to feel you are leaving work behind you is vitally important, even if your job doesn't entail the extremes that hers did, especially when there aren't visible, physical cues for you, like a car ride or bus trip home. A study of work commutes found that, for their sample of people, the "ideal" commute time was 16 minutes: long enough feel that they had left work behind but not so long that it was burdensome.[131] That transition time, it turns out, is important, and it tells our deep mind that *something is ending, and something else is beginning.* Leaving for work. Coming home. Taking off a jacket and hanging it up.

CLEANSING—WASHING OFF THE DAY

It's hard to overstate the universality of water as a symbol of change and renewal. If a liminal ritual tells us that we are moving from one world to another, then water signals that *we ourselves are changed.* From the baptism of Christians to the Hindus' holy bath in the river Ganges, or the cleansing water of the Orthodox Jews' Mikvah pool, humans seem to understand that water doesn't wash off only worldly dirt and grime but emotional and spiritual residue as well.

When I first started in private practice, I found myself absorbed in the stories and emotions of my clients, more than I had ever experienced before. When you work at a community mental health agency, you usually don't spend the same number of hours connecting deeply with clients—there's just not the time or the opportunity. I think there's also a buffer in the constant interaction with colleagues. An agency usually has a place to distract yourself with gossip, to grab lunch and talk about anything other than work, and to discharge immediately any self-doubt or distressing feelings that a session may have brought up. You can go over things with a supervisor, or even just pop into somebody's office for a quick debriefing or reassuring hug. In a private practice office, it's harder to come by those things. For many of us, most of the time, we're alone while we're inundated with the pain of our clients. Sometimes it can feel like drowning.

So, I was grappling with more intense clients and spending more in-depth time with them, without my usual guardrails. I had learned how to hold and manage the strong emotions of clients, but now I had to find new ways to set them down again. At the end of a workweek, I noticed that I worried about my clients—about how I had done with them, moments I missed or fumbled. Most of all, their stories and pain tended to bang around in my head. I ruminated on the nightmares they described and felt some of the terror they felt waking up from them. I imagined myself, or people I love, living through what they had endured. I fretted about how my clients would fare between sessions, if a situation they were struggling with would be better or worse the next time I saw them. It was too much distress, and I knew, from my training but also from my gut, that I wouldn't last long if I didn't find a way to let things go. Coincidentally, I had started going to the Ohio State student athletic center to swim on Fridays after work.[132] I realized that I was sort-of-consciously trying to tell myself to let things go while I swam laps in my incredibly slow backstroke (I personally prefer to describe my pace as "dignified").

Once I noticed that I was doing this, I began to take it more seriously. I would think over the week, send each client a wish for their well-being, and then imagine, with each lap, the pool washing away the stories I'd heard. Now I know that the coordinated movement of my arms and legs probably helped regulate my brain, and the effort released serotonin, helping to clear away the stress chemicals my brain had been soaked in that week. By the time I was done and showering off the chlorine (more cleansing), I was tired—and peaceful. The thoughts about my clients might still pop up, but it was much easier to gently move them to the Monday Morning Box in my head. And that is how I would know that the weekend, my break from therapy world, had begun.[133]

Obviously, there are both cleansing and liminal images going on here, but it's the water that is central to this story.

Transcendence—Connecting to Infinity

"The experience of infinity should not be confused with eternity. Eternity means an endless number of days. Eternity is bound to time, to be growing old and dying. Infinity is prior to time itself and existed before time was born. And since infinity was never born, it is undying."

—*Alberto Villoldo*, Shaman, Healer, Sage

You may have heard the Japanese phrase "forest bathing," which, I'm sure, is at best a fraction of the meaning in the original. I often find myself recommending forest bathing to my (somewhat surprised) clients. When I mean is: *Go to where trees and grass and animals are, then let yourself really feel them. Listen to sounds other than the ones human beings make. Smell the dirt and the dry leaves, and watch the light and shadows move on the blades of grass.*

Does this "bath" magically solve your problems? Nope. You'll leave the trees and walk out of the park, or backyard, or garden, and meet the same struggles you dropped off at the entrance when you came in. But it does provide something humans often miss, as we live our lives walled off in moving boxes (cars) and standing boxes (buildings) in our artificial, unfeeling new skins (clothing). Nature reconnects us to what is bigger than we are. It reminds us that not only are our problems small, lasting mere seconds in the great ages of the earth, but also that things have a deeper structure and a constant, communicating framework of which we are not usually aware. This structure carries on blissfully without us. Birds don't need our direction to build their nests, and trees are perfectly content to grow in their own unique form, scraggly bits and all, without our criticism or encouragement or staff meetings or strategic plans.

It can be soothing to remember that *none* of this needs your help. If you can fill your lungs with air and feel the grass under your feet, you might even get that fleeting reminder that you are also a part of all this, a tiny fiber woven into the living net that is draped over our planet. Your lungs and skin and bones and blood emerged from the same molecules as the dirt and the plants and will return to them again. You really are not separate from it at all, though it can feel like you are. It strikes me when I happen across a home decorating show (we are very attached to our boxes and like to make them pretty!) that manages to work in the cliché of "bringing the outdoors inside" by virtue of the radical act of placing a potted plant in a room. I remind myself, "I don't have to bring nature inside. I am nature, myself, and I am inside already."

In other words, you don't have to go to nature. You *are* nature. It's just that sometimes, we little bits of nature are too cut off from the bigger pieces of nature for too long, and it helps our minds and hearts to slide back into place and rest. We can just be, breathing along with every other living thing for a moment or two.

Communion—Find Your People

Community organizer John McKnight said that "circle is the shape of community."[134] When I discussed ritual in my classes, I often used the quintessential circle of trust—12-Step meetings. It's true that some bigger meetings are arranged in rows of seats rather than a circle, but the circle is an enduring image for the community experience of being, quite literally, among your people. Twelve-Step meetings use many ritual elements, and like all good rituals, they are highly repetitive. Not every chapter does everything exactly like another, but the major traditions are the same, and each meeting follows a similar routine to leave one time and place behind, enter another to do special work, and then leave to rejoin the flow of daily life:

Prepare to leave the ordinary world: (milling about, getting coffee, chatting, etc.) and enter the special world of the meeting

Form the circle: sit, introduce yourself/formally recognize others, state the purpose of this special work in this special place

Do the work of the meeting: emotions, stories, readings, support, affirmation

End the work of the meeting: slogans, prayers, reiteration of community, and protecting it with the rule of confidentiality before the breaking of the circle

Prepare to reenter the daily world: (more milling about, more coffee, hugs)

Say goodbye and exit

Similar ritual progressions can be seen in mosques at prayer, synagogues every Friday night, and in churches every Sunday morning. The formula is largely the same: Leave the world, enter into a special space to do special things, reaffirm lasting connection as you break the space to enter the world again. This is the deep story we watched Mister Rogers perform, again and again. We can find lesser forms in the ritualized format of a yoga class or a book club—the vestiges are still there.

You do not have to connect with people only in these settings, of course, but I have noticed that when we do not have some form of this ritualized recognition of space, connection, and purpose, the power of connection is weaker, and the effect fades faster. For some people, consumerism is a substitute for all this, but commerce is the opposite of communion. Let's say you get hungry, and you want to buy yourself some lunch. You enter a McDonald's alone. You are there only to take, and you leave with something only for yourself. No one marks your coming or going (other than the robotic greeting of the cashier), and you are expected to conduct only your personal business and be on your way. It's fine if you want a hamburger, but you will not be fed on any other level. Find a place to connect with humans in a deeper way, and you will experience more of the benefits.

For those of us who feel we are drowning already in the thoughts and feelings of others, communion with human beings may feel like the last thing you want to do, and you may be right. You may need solitude for cleansing and reflecting, passing from one world to another. But you may feel different enough in these community settings to make it worth it to you: not the fixer, the leader, the helper, the knower, but only the grateful participant, a sharer of the small world you have created together, for a time, to do work with some authentic purpose.

Rituals can also be a part of your workday. In *The Way Through*, I mention the quick check-in we did before every shift change. This was at my first social work job, and it was among the many things I have brought with me wherever I could throughout my professional career. A quick check-in circle helps to ground everyone and gives them a little moral support from their teammates when needed, so they can set their personal lives aside for a while and focus more effectively on the day. I think any version of this that you can create with your team is powerful.

If you don't work around other people, that's OK, because you can do the same thing on your own. I know many therapists who pause to do a few minutes of meditation before they start their day, or they say a fast, silent prayer or affirmation before walking in to start a session. You could take a few minutes to quickly tidy your workspace at the end of the day (and I mean *really quickly*—lining up the edges of your stacks of Post-Its counts! No one is talking deep cleaning here) and reflecting on the day, letting yourself know it's done. One practitioner I know makes a point at the end of her day to connect with her Higher Power to refresh herself and feel grateful for any help she feels she's received. Whatever is most meaningful to you will work best.

Rituals, as we've said, are the retelling or the reshowing of a story over and over again. The repetition gives the story power and depth. Another word for story here could be "truth." So, ask yourself, as you think about the rituals you might incorporate into your work and your day, what stories do I need to strengthen for myself again and again? What truths do I want to reinforce? They might sound something like:

I exist beyond what I offer to other people.

My being is precious and worth caring for.

My body is a marvel and worth protecting.

I am more than this body, even while I cherish it.

I am more than this job, even while I value it.

I am more than this caretaking role, even while I inhabit it gladly.

I am more than the people I love and who love me, even while I love them.

I am more than how people perceive me.

My work will be OK left here for a while until I pick it up again.

Help is available to me; I am not struggling alone.

I am part of all of Life on this Earth, and I have a place in it.

There is a bigger picture, and I am a small part of it, not the center on which everything rests or depends.

I am not missing or lacking anything.

This moment contains within it the potential for everything it needs.

CHAPTER ELEVEN

Seven Hours and Three Meals: A Folktale

"What is to give light must endure burning."

—*Viktor Frankl*

Years ago, I read a profile about a young physician's experience volunteering to provide disaster relief with Doctors Without Borders. He wrote that when he was first considering joining, he read the program requirements, which included agreeing to eat three meals a day and to sleep at least seven hours every night while on assignment. He was concerned about what serving would mean to his life and his career, the challenge and the opportunity, not the small organizational rules and regulations along the way, so he didn't pay a lot of attention to this, and he forgot about them pretty much immediately afterwards. He started filling out detailed forms and meeting representatives for interviews. At some point in the application process, the eat-three-meals-and-sleep-seven-hours thing was mentioned again, and as a doctor, he thought, *Sure, good suggestion for anybody. Whatever.* Finally, after being accepted and getting ready to leave for his tour, he was reminded once again that he had to eat three meals a day and sleep seven hours a night; once again, he promised, thinking, *OK, already! Man, they sure are making a big deal out of commonsense medical advice.*

And then he arrived in Haiti. It was 2010.

A 7.0 earthquake and its aftershocks had just ripped apart cities and villages. The chaos that follows a disaster had done its grim work next, stalking through the population with fires, violence, and disease. The result was misery he had never imagined. Basic services were unavailable, major roads were impassable, and drinking water was contaminated. In his telling, the people in the surrounding areas would walk for hours to reach the medical clinic, and some stayed camped out overnight if they couldn't get in that day. Some had headed out well before first light to get there. He quickly realized that no matter how early they opened the clinic doors, people would already be lined up to get in. No matter how many patients they treated, they would end up closing the door in someone's face at the end of the day, and the ones left waiting would have to choose between a night sleeping by the clinic steps or trudging the long miles back home, only to return and try again the next day.

He and the other clinic doctors and nurses could have worked endlessly, worked themselves to death, and it would not have been enough. They still would not have been able to see all the people and provide all the help they wanted to offer. He understood for the first time that if he did not diligently take care of himself, eating and sleeping and taking breaks and connecting and unwinding with his coworkers at the end of the day, then he might well end up driving himself to his own physical collapse—and all *that* would mean was that the clinic staff would have one more person to take care of. Maybe they would just drag his unconscious body out of the way and prop him in a corner to come to on his own while they attended to more urgent cases. Nobody wanted to do that. More to the point: Nobody had time for it.

In a way, working themselves past their limits was now a luxury, one that none of them could afford anymore. What they were doing was simply too important, and a melodramatic crash from neglecting his own needs would be swept away in the tidal wave of suffering they were fighting.

I have told this story as I remember it for many years now. If I get some of the details wrong, it probably doesn't matter anymore because for me, it's become a fable for all the helping professions; a cautionary tale to be told around the campfire. When I taught social work to graduate students, I always made sure to tell it at some point in the semester, no matter what the course was, because I felt passionately that this truth was simply not emphasized enough by the college, though they tried. I had worked in the field for some time by then, and I had confronted a little of the world's great destruction and pain myself. I knew that social work, like all the other helping professions, faces disaster every day—not as dramatic as the devastation of an earthquake on a Caribbean island, maybe, but certainly as relentless.

I always wrapped up my little campfire story with a moral: There is no limit to the suffering in the world, and if you want to give up your own well-being to it, you can go right ahead. No one will stop you. You can fling yourself into the volcano of overwork and neglect of self and never be heard from again. Not only will this not end the suffering, but also, I promise you: *The world will not even notice.* If you destroy yourself mentally or physically, the program you work for will simply hire someone else; the clients you serve will still show up the next day to be seen (but not by you); the schools will turn out newly minted social workers every spring, and your sacrifice will mean nothing to anyone but you. Think hard and make your choices. What we undertake to do with our lives as helpers can be deadly serious, and it is not for amateurs or romantics.

We have to decide what *our* "three meals and seven hours" will be: how we will preserve and nurture ourselves in the face of all that we confront every day. For me, one more sacrificial skeleton on the volcano floor is not noble. It's just a waste.

CHAPTER TWELVE

Your Body, Electric: Taking Care of Your Instrument

"O my Body! I dare not desert the likes of you."

—Walt Whitman, *I Sing the Body Electric*

So much of the work of healing trauma is in the body, and we are learning more almost daily about the indivisible body, brain, and psyche. One book can't possibly cover it all, including this one, but we'll go just a little further and talk in this chapter about the physical side of the self. We'll take a quick look at the ways many of us can neglect our bodies—either in an attempt to escape the feelings they hold, or simply because we're so busy paying attention to the care of others that we've forgotten our own wellness. As I'll say many more times, there is no medical advice here—just gentle reminders about what bodies usually need and how we might reconnect with them through our own nurturing and care.

As we continue to think about reconnecting with the world by reconnecting with ourselves, it helps to understand how the vessel of the self—the body—works and how it responds to stress, sometimes turning it into inflammation and disease. We have to have a body that works to be here on Earth, among other people.

There's probably nothing I need to tell you about how to take care of your body. If this is something that is important to you, you already read health tips and listen to lots of suggestions. There may be some interesting information here to think about, or you might want to skip this chapter.

But maybe this is an area you've neglected lately. If you haven't been taking care of your body for a while, it's OK to begin now. If you're going to make any big changes, *you need to see a doctor first;* this book is not a replacement for individualized medical advice. And don't worry, in the next chapter, we'll talk about how to start, if that is intimidating. But I do want to tell you a little about what we are learning about the relationship between mind, brain, body, and stress.

First, Gabor Maté has several books that I've quoted from, especially from his most recent one, *The Myth of Normal.* Second only to Van der Kolk's *The Body Keeps the Score,* this is the book I recommend most often to my clients, particularly if they are dealing with pain, illness, or other physical problems that may be related in some part to stress. So, let's talk about stress.

Lots of people have told you, in lots of ways, that stress is bad. But as usual, the real story of stress is more complicated. In *The Way Through,* I talk a little about cortisol, the stress hormone that runs through us, binding to receptor sites found everywhere throughout our bodies, and I point out that, like everything in our bodies, cortisol serves an important function. We need it, or it would be hard to do things like stand up or move around.[135]

In fact, stress is such a general term that it's not very useful, so I'll break it down a little. There are actually two kinds of stress. *Eustress* means effort or tension toward something good. The physical version of it is often compared to working out. When you lift a weight over and over, you stress the muscle, making it work hard; so hard, in fact, that it tears the muscle fibers a tiny bit. Then, when it heals itself, the tissues that have filled in to repair the tear make the muscle bulkier and stronger. That's why muscles get bigger; we literally tear them down a little to make them grow. The stress on them makes them stronger in the long run. Emotionally, *eustress* is probably most likely felt in times of hard work that we enjoy or feel successful at.

Even after decades of public speaking, I still get nervous before I go out to face an audience. This is pretty amazing considering that I am an incurable ham.[136] In those moments of jitters before I begin and in the intense effort of keeping track of what I'm saying, whether the audience is engaged or bored, and how much time I have to wrap it all up, the experience of speaking is stressful. But it plays to my strengths, it's important, and I enjoy it even though I have to work hard to do it well. Like a muscle being worked, I build resilience and confidence after each strain. That is *eustress*.

Then there's *distress*. Well, I hardly need to spell it out for you at this point; it's the opposite of all the things I just said. This is the bad kind of stress. When we lack tools and skills ... when we fear failing ... when we're frustrated and overwhelmed—that's when we experience the stress that demoralizes us and causes damage in the long term. There's no enjoyment in the process, just dread and drudgery. As we talked about from the beginning of *The Way Through,* we're built for work, and for danger. Our ancient ancestors spent plenty of time doing hard, scary, or boring things, from hunting (and sometimes being hunted by) powerful animals or the backbreaking labor of gathering and farming. We can handle distress, even intense distress—to a point.

In so many classic explanations of trauma, it boils down to the same message—we are built to do this (tolerate stress, deal with a threat, etc.) *in small doses* or quick bursts that happen rarely. We are not meant to live with that worry, fear, and powerlessness day in, day out. I genuinely think being chased by a tiger once is better for our mental health than having a regular job in which we feel powerless, devalued, and frustrated daily. The tiger causes us a quick, terrified burst of adrenaline, and then when it's over, it's over. We get to rest in a tree (or later in our history, in our small village), congratulating ourselves on our clever escape. We probably savor our food a little more than usual that night, appreciate a comfy bed, and have a great story to tell around the cooking pit. But it's hard to picture primordial men and women sitting around listlessly, dreading Monday morning week after week, month after month, year after year.

This is not an endorsement for being attacked by tigers; it's simply to say that what modern medicine seems to be telling us with study after study is that *chronic, grinding stress is bad for us,* and I can only conclude that we really weren't built for it. Ideally, we would find sources of eustress, likely starting with some of the qualities I talked about in the chapter about Flow, and experience distress the way we were supposed to—an occasional thing, not the life we're meant to live every day.

Interestingly, cortisol can signal danger in more than one way: high levels of stress can be markers that we are under too much stress too often. But Maté points out that when our cortisol levels are *too* low, that can mean that stress has gotten worse. " . . . [C]ortisol levels can indicate problems when out of range in both directions: lower cortisol can be bad sign that is a marker of long-term stress: a sign that people's healthy, protective stress-response mechanism [is] burning out."[137]

Yet another way to explain the problems at both ends of the stress spectrum is "allostatic load." This is one of the mechanisms of allostasis: *allo* means "other" or "from outside," and *stasis* means stability or continuity. So, *allostasis* is how our bodies, these systems of nerves and blood and fluid that are contained in our skins, deal with the environment they're walking around in. When you think about it, it's amazing (or terrifying) that a few thin layers of tissue keep all our organs held together and protected from the entire world. Our systems have unimaginably clever ways to monitor and maintain us, which I discuss in *The Way Through*.

To keep from getting too far off course into a discussion of medical theory, I'll go back to our example of a house. A house's main job is to keep the outside *outside*, using walls, floor, and ceiling. For humans to live in it, the house must protect us from the elements and maintain breathable air and suitable temperatures inside. Its foundation can't slide around, and the ceiling has to stay waterproof. Because it has these requirements, your house has ways of checking itself, and in some cases, adjusting when things are out of range. Mold growing in your basement tells you water is getting in through the walls. A smoke detector and carbon monoxide monitor check the air to make sure there is enough oxygen and only trace amounts of poisonous gases or you'll die. The thermostat checks the temperature constantly, making sure it stays in the range you set.

Your body works essentially the same way, so allostasis is how your house stays upright, keeps the water and wind outside and conditions livable and comfortable inside. Allostatic load is the burden of doing it—all the energy your house uses to do this. In a blizzard or a heat wave, your house has to work harder. If your house is exposed to lightning strikes and snowstorms and sharknadoes, there's more damage, and you have to do more upkeep. In fact, the typical layperson definition of allostatic load is "wear-and-tear from stress," like the wear-and-tear on your house over the years of standing upright in the elements. In *The Myth of Normal,* Maté talks about this concept:

> First, its physiology and consequences include the acute or chronic activation, potential overactivation, and even

exhaustion of the hypothalamic-pituitary-adrenal (HPA) axis that connects our brain's emotional centers and the body's entire physiological apparatus. Then there is what Bruce McEwen has called 'allostatic load': the wear and tear on the body of having to maintain its internal equilibrium in the face of changing and challenging circumstances, trauma salient among them . . .

He points out that in our current state, this is an increasing problem for us. "In this culture many people are fated to be bearers of heavy allostatic loads, to the detriment of their mental and physical health . . . "[138]

SOCIAL STRESSORS

The "many people" he refers to is a wider circle than those of us in the helping professions. I've listed a few of the high-risk groups he mentions:

- indigenous people
- economically stressed people
- urban-dwelling people
- people of color (living in historically white-majority cultures)
- people in over-stressed, under-supported jobs (of any profession)
- female people

If you are in more than one of these categories, the chronic (dis)stress goes up, as does the damage it brings with it. One way it impacts us is that our bodies literally age faster. This happens when our telomeres get shorter. Telomeres are like little strands that cap the ends of our cells, and our cells use them to reproduce themselves. The shorter these strands get, the fewer times a cell can replace itself. An explanation of this: " . . . [e]very time a cell in our body divides, the telomeres shorten; when they get too short, their host cell dies or may deteriorate and become dysfunctional. As they shrink, immune function is impaired, inflammation rises and we fall more prone to illness . . . *stress shortens telomeres* [emphasis mine]"[139]

This may mean that our daily grind really *is* grinding us down. The good news is that it appears we can slow down the shortening of the telomeres. Some genes in our bodies may be malleable; in other words, we can turn them "on" with environmental factors, including stress, kicking off some disease processes. And in some cases, when we reduce the stress, we turn that gene "off" again or at least, in the case of telomeres, slow down how fast we're using them up.

This should also make you think about things some of us have to deal with and others do not, such as racism, ableism, homophobia, anti-immigrant hatred, and on and on.

When researchers compared telomere length, for example, Black women were on average seven years "older" than white women, and this is "consistent with higher rates of poverty, stress, hypertension [high blood pressure], obesity and related health conditions. "'Our findings literally suggest that racism makes people old."[140]

PEOPLE-PLEASING

"An unusually perceptive Canadian specialist . . . wrote
in 1957 that his patients with RA [rheumatoid arthritis]
'usually tried very hard to please both in professional and
personal contacts, and either concealed hostility or expressed
it indirectly. Many were perfectionistic.'"
—Gabor Maté, *The Myth of Normal*

This trait is not new to most of you reading this book; it would be hard to find professions less likely to attract people-pleasers than the helping professions. So, what's the difference between helping and pleasing? I think there are two ways to think about this. One is simple: We just look back at our previous chapter about the Three Empathies. When we are triggered or dysregulated at work, let's say, this may send us into hyper-arousal, the "Four Fs." Remember what the fourth F is? It's *Fawning;* moving closer to a threat to neutralize it and restore our feeling of safety. Usually, the threat we're dealing with is an angry person. Fawning is a pretty close synonym for people-pleasing, but it's also a pattern of behavior that may go well beyond simply placating someone in the moment.

Some of us are people-pleasers who habitually overcommit, overdo, over fix, over care, and over offer ourselves. We may spend hours obsessing over someone at work being slightly disappointed or upset, regardless of how questionable their gripe is or how indirectly we were the cause of their feelings. I think that when we're not people-pleasing it's easier to help more objectively, and to take things less personally if something doesn't work out or if someone is unhappy.

I know; it takes a lot of thought and discernment to figure out if you're helping or pleasing. Another way to talk about this is our inability to figure out if we're feeling "guilt" from actually having done something wrong or if we're merely taking on the feelings of others, as we may have learned to do as children. You may have been taught to "metabolize" the emotions of other people, either directly or indirectly. I had a friend who would be told, when his father was isolating in his room during one of his periods of dark depression, to "go in and apologize to him." Despite not having done anything wrong and certainly nothing that would cause depression in an adult (because that's not a thing), my friend would trudge in and do this. He was, quite literally, a child told to take responsibility for the feelings of a grown-up.

For others, this type of response may have been something learned simply as self-protection. If you took responsibility for monitoring and "fixing things," calming things down when someone else was upset, then maybe you got to feel safe, at least for the moment. But this is a distortion. Later in life, if we feel that we're not "fixing" someone enough, we confuse that feeling of dread ("I'm not safe") with a feeling of guilt ("I should be doing more so they'll feel better," etc.). It's really fear that we're feeling, and so the guilt is misplaced. Guilt is what we should feel when we violate our personal norms or ethics—that's what it's for, and in that original sense, it's a useful emotion to help us live up to our own values. Feeling other people's feelings for them, anticipating and managing them for that person, was never our job; it's not something we owe anybody.

If you're someone who misidentifies dread as guilt, it can help to clarify things by gently asking yourself, "Did I actually do anything that violates my ethics or morals? Or am I maybe just afraid of this person's anger or punishment for not doing enough caretaking or placating them? Is 'dread' a better word than 'guilt' for this feeling right now?"

Suppressing or misdirecting emotions can be linked to changes in the body. Again, we'll quote Gabor Maté, since the influence of emotional stress on the body is what he has largely built his work on in the past decade:

> Body and mind, while not identical, cannot be understood separately from each other . . . a 1965 survey reported the prevalence in rheumatoid arthritis-prone individuals of an array of self-abnegating traits: a "compulsive and self-sacrificing doing for others, suppression of anger, and excessive concerns about social acceptability."[141]

Paying attention to all the feelings and indicators in this book might help you figure out if you're people-pleasing.

PATHOLOGICAL SELF-RELIANCE

Next, we're going to talk about over-coping and relying on ourselves alone as a reaction to stress. And yep, this can be hard to distinguish from plain old coping, which many helpers are already extremely good at in their jobs. I think that, once again, thinking about how childhood felt for us might offer some clues here.

So many of my clients are very intelligent, highly accomplished people. In our culture, we value "achievement" so much that I think we rarely stop to ask where all that achievement is coming from, or more simply, *exactly why this person is so good at doing so much, for so much longer than the average person.* We certainly don't ask very often about the toll it takes on them. We usually assume that the rewards (praise, money, status) make up for whatever price they pay for all their effort. It's true that there are differences in individuals, and some people have a naturally higher drive than others. No one, though, is naturally able to do everything by themselves, with no support, forever.

Back to my clients: many of them struggle terribly to genuinely give up control to others, to rely on the people around them for real help, or to let anyone see them truly vulnerable. In the words of Chapter Four, they find it almost impossible to be strong like a willow. It's too scary to bend. This is often because they grew up feeling that it's safer to be alone—even though many of these people now have loving families, admiring friends, and endless praise from coworkers or colleagues. They are shocked to hear themselves described as "alone," but that stance of '*No one can see me weak, no one can know all my flaws, and no one can be truly relied upon but myself*' is, I would argue, a profound state of isolation. So many of us can be described with these terms: hyperfunctioning, hyper-responsible, pathologically self-reliant, or self-sufficient. *Pathological* here is meant in its most objective medical sense: Our reliance only on self comes from, and results in, injury or illness. Maté talks about the result of living our lives this way:

> One no longer knows one's body. Oddly, this self-estrangement can show up later in life as an apparent strength, such as my ability to perform on a high level when hungry or stressed or fatigued, pushing on without the awareness of any need for pause, nutrition or rest. Alternatively, some people's disconnection from their bodies manifests as not knowing when to stop eating or drinking—the "enough" signal doesn't get through.[142]

When therapists talk about body awareness, or as I recently heard it called, "body literacy," we're often talking about this state that many of us find ourselves frozen into, and like any estrangement, we may dearly miss what we've lost.

Speaking of hyper-self-reliance, some helpers struggle to admit they need even basic medical care. Add to that the fact that doctors and nurses and nurse practitioners face unprecedented demand with fewer resources, and it can be a real challenge to find medical support. You might be reluctant to look for a new medical practice even if you don't like or feel uncomfortable with your current care providers. I get it. I talk with clients about this all the time, and I never want to add one more thing to your to-do list. Take your time if you need to; get help finding resources if you need to. *But,* I always go on to say, *you deserve a doctor you like and trust.* I am going to strongly ask, urge, badger, and bug you to get good medical care. You and your body deserve it.

INNATE SENSITIVITY

There are some of us who may be born with heightened sensitivity to stress. Maté calls those of us "orchids":

> [E]xquisitely sensitive to their environment, making them especially vulnerable under conditions of adversity but unusually vital, creative, and successful within supportive, nurturing environments. The same "sensitivity" gene that in a stressed environment can help potentiate mental suffering may, under positive circumstances, help promote stronger mental resilience and therefore happiness. Sensitive people have the potential to be more aware, insightful, inventive, artistic, and *empathic* [emphasis mine], if their sensitivity is not crushed by maltreatment or disdain.[143]

Sensitivity is perhaps both a gift and a curse, but there is pressure on women, regardless of our inborn sensitivity or lack of it, that also puts us at risk. All women are constantly expected to be attuned to others, so along with other social stressors I mentioned earlier, we may be ageing and getting sick faster that we should. This process has an internal engine: inflammation. Inflammation is the call coming from inside the house.

Inflammation is "a signature marker of stress . . . implicated in an extensive range of pathologies, from autoimmune conditions to vascular disease of heart and brain, from cancer to depression. 'A theme that comes up over and over again is this increase in inflammatory gene activity in people confronting a sense of threat or insecurity for more than a short period of time. We can detect these same markers in mice, in monkeys. As far down as in fish, you can see that the more stress or threat or uncertainty you're exposed to, the more the body turns on this defense mechanism that involves more inflammation.'"[144] In fact, we are learning that inflammation is so central to all of these processes that understanding how it works may be the next revolution in mental and medical sciences.

ANGELS, ASSASSINS, AND ELECTRICITY IN YOUR BRAIN

"I sing the body electric."

—Walt Whitman, *I Sing the Body Electric*

As we talk about inflammation, it may help to catch up with the latest ideas about how exactly inflammation in your body could be affecting your brain. In her fascinating book, *The Angel and the Assassin,* Donna Jackson Nakazawa tells the stories of several women dealing with intense anxiety and depression. She takes us through innovative nonpharmaceutical treatments to help these conditions and introduces us to the even bigger story: groundbreaking discoveries about how the brain may shift from managing inflammation to increasing it. When we talk about stress being the factor that "turns on" illnesses, scientists may have found the on-switch.[145]

Nakazawa explains our new understanding of the role of microglials,[146] led by the discoveries of neuroscientist Beth Stevens. The microglials are the smallest brain cells we have, and, up until now, probably the least interesting. In this book and my last one, along with countless others, understanding the brain has usually focused on the neurons. Neurons carry the "electrical activity" of the brain, and we often talk about them as wires or networks. Glial cells are usually not terribly relevant to the average reader. Until now. Glial cells are like the gelatin of the brain: If your brain were a Jell-O mold, then everyone's favorites—the fruit pieces—are the neurons; the glia are the gelatin surrounding the pieces in place and holding them in place. There are four types of glial cells.[147] Microglials are the smallest of these four types, and up until recently, we understood them mostly as tiny dump trucks for the brain, carting away the debris of cells that have died. Useful, but not very interesting. Now we may have a completely new understanding that puts them at the center of the health and well-being of the brain.

Dr. Stevens got stubbornly interested in a cell we hadn't paid much attention to and found out that microglials have a much more active role than mere housekeeping; they actually have a dual nature and flip back and forth between these two versions of themselves. Microglia check all our brain cells all the time, sending out tiny little filaments to interact with the other brain cells. Nakazawa describes them as "tapping" on each brain cell, like you'd tap a melon to see if it's ripe. If the brain cell seems healthy, the microglia behave angelically, releasing nurturing chemicals that help strengthen and sustain that healthy cell. If they tap and the cell seems sickly, they send out destructive chemicals that move things along to cell death, like teeny assassins, and then cart the remains away.

This would all be interesting to the average brain nerd like me but not terribly relevant to this book if the story ended here. It doesn't.

These unassuming microglial cells might drive the brain's immune system. Just like our bodies' immune systems, when something is wrong, inflammation creates the fever or the swelling that helps us repel invaders and restore our systems to equilibrium. The catch is that, up until very recently, we believed that the brain itself didn't *have* an immune system. The discoveries Stevens and others are putting together say that it does, in fact, and that microglia may be its key.

The hypothesis is that when the body is inflamed, it signals distress through lymphatic channels (that we also didn't think the brain had!). Your body has lymph nodes everywhere. When you get a checkup, and the doctor feels along just under your jaw, she is checking to see if the lymph nodes (usually small and soft) are swollen with lymphatic fluid. If they are, it means your immune system has been activated, and you may have an infection. This might also trigger redness and irritation throughout your body as white blood cells and other soldiers of your immune system assemble to fight off invading bacteria or viruses.

"Autoimmune" diseases, then, are diseases in which our immune systems start attacking us for no reason and damage healthy cells instead of killing invading bacteria or viruses. With the discovery of these lymph channels into the brain, we may have found the hidden passageway that messengers of trouble in the body communicate directly with the brain. These messages go to microglials, and suddenly the angels fall from grace. Now, instead of helping sick cells die, they turn on healthy cells and start killing *them* off, too. Just like in the body, the immune system of the brain goes berserk and starts killing randomly. The full moon that causes the switch from mild-mannered to killer is likely the brain's response to inflammation, and that might all be starting in the body.[148]

If these hypotheses stand up to more study, and the neuroscientists at the heart of this revolution think that they will, we may see a revolution in psychiatry, neurology, and immunology. Nakazawa describes a future where we talk about inflammation and Parkinson's, Alzheimer's, schizophrenic disorders, depression, anxiety, and more. "Psycho-neuro-immunology" is going to be a pain to spell, but it might be the name of our next integrative medical specialty, and many of our clients have a real stake in its potential. As Dr. Hasan Asif put it in *The Angel and the Assassin*, "This is very hopeful news for the fields of psychiatry, psychoanalysis [sic], immunology and neuroscience . . .

because it shows us that these seemingly disparate fields are *one field* [emphasis mine]. And if we combine our knowledge, we will almost certainly be able to help more patients heal."[149]

The Angel and the Assassin goes on to outline the anti-inflammatory treatments that made extraordinary changes for the patients whose stories the author follows. Medication-resistant mood issues transform, seemingly like magic, for the patients in the book. Anxiety becomes manageable instead of paralyzing, and depression lifts. It seems that treating inflammation in the brain resets microglial functioning, and the cells appear to go back to their angelic selves, helping where they can and killing only when necessary.[150]

I chose to write about all this because I think this new science has something to offer us, not just professionally but personally as well. Let's start with the professional. If Dr. Asif is right, the microglial connection may also explain why gut health (and remember, the gut is the only place besides your brain that has neural cells in it; that's why doctors sometimes call our gut "the second brain") is emerging as a major factor in our mental and neurological health. If this is true, then getting serious about reducing inflammatory foods in our clients' diets, getting serious about encouraging exercise, and getting serious about addressing trauma and stress in our clients' lives may have a direct impact on their brains. If we can help to reduce brain inflammation, we might see improvement in neurological disorders, psychiatric disorders, and more run-of-the-mill mood problems as well. If we can ask about nonpharmacological treatments like transcranial magnetic stimulation or neurofeedback for our individuals, we may see some of the gains Nakazawa describes, possibly reducing the need for some of the heavy-hitting psychotropics that can be hard to tolerate and come with real neurological risks. If we can test for Alzheimer's and other dementia-related diseases, we can protect brains already compromised by developmental disabilities.

Now take all of these potential benefits and apply them to yourself. That's the personal part.

For me, part of the appeal of the microglial story is all the scientists who were the primary players making the leaps to recognize the maybe crucial role microglials play. Nakazawa talks with an array of professionals and, of course, credits the men whose research or treatment innovations move the story along. But many of the stars here are women, including the young scientist who developed imaging sensitive enough to capture the movement of microglia, showing their floating, delicate filaments in action in real time, checking on cells and then either helping or hurting them.[151]

There's something poetically just about all this for any helping professional, but especially for those of us who serve the least regarded in our society: We often concern ourselves with people who have been written off as insignificant or even invisible. Many of us (though certainly not all) are women, and I'm probably not spoiling any secrets for you when I tell you that women, and the professional fields traditionally associated with them, *also* tend to be overlooked, undervalued, and poorly paid. How fitting if it turns out that "the least of these" in our brains are, in fact, terribly important after all. Our bodies are every bit as exciting—as *electric*—as Walt Whitman said they were.

Nutrition

Food is usually fairly simple. Eating is not. See if you can find ways to allow comfort, pleasure, fuel, presence, and self-care to all be parts of how you eat.

Sleep

Well, it's more important than we ever thought. It's not that waking is the default and sleep is the lesser state. Recent research about sleep suggests that trauma can cause sleep problems, and sleep problems make trauma symptoms worse.[152] A friend of mine who is a general practitioner routinely talks about targeting sleep as the first line of working on depression and anxiety; or, as she says to her patients, "If you aren't sleeping, mood is a hole you just can't climb out of."

In my experience, many of us live with ongoing sleep problems. If someone said to you, "I am doubled over in pain every day," you'd be driving them to an emergency room, or at least you'd be very concerned about them. But clients will routinely tell me that they sleep less than six hours, wake up throughout the night or early every morning before they need to, or that a spouse wakes them with snoring, and that this happens almost every night. For years. And when I suggest talking to a doctor, they shrug as if to say, "Yeah, I know, but I can handle it." Nope! They can't. No brain can handle that. We may get used to trudging along, but that's not the same thing. The more we learn about inflammation in the brain and body, the more we see that without the clearing away and restoration of sleep, our brains just can't do as well as we want them to.

Here is a list of things you probably know you should be doing:

Try to get at least seven consecutive hours a night.

Sleep in a cool room. Your body temperature needs to drop about a degree for you to fall asleep and stay asleep at night. Now I'm going to talk about a very touchy subject, and that is . . . dogs. I'm really sorry, guys, but apart from the eternal dogs-in-the-bed debate among trainers, there's another reason why letting dogs sleep with you might be a bad idea. I've worked with many people over the years who tell me their sleep is disrupted all night, and they're too hot to drift off. When

I ask, "Do you have dogs in bed with you?" they look away guiltily and say some version of "I know, but I can't help it!" Or that they have a spouse who insists on having the dogs in bed with them. Here's the thing. Having had dogs myself, I get it. But if we agree with my doctor friend that without restful sleep, nothing else can get better, then you see where we are. The dogs will make a fuss, your partner might make a fuss, but if you are overly heated and/or disturbed by dogs in bed, it's really time to think about changing this practice.

Avoid:

- looking at a screen within an hour of trying to fall asleep
- falling asleep with a TV on
- drinking too much caffeine too late in the day
- going to bed at widely varied times
- snoring
- sleeping with a partner who snores

If you have any, some, or all of these habits, I promise there is no judgment when I say that the single best thing you can do to help your health starting *today* (assuming you aren't doing obviously damaging things like hard drugs or ignoring a major health issue like untreated high blood pressure, etc.) is to work on your sleep.

Start:

- turning the heat down a bit at night, or use a fan
- using a comfy sleep mask to make sure things are dark enough
- going to bed within an hour of the same time every night
- ending screen time within an hour of bedtime

Progress to:
- cutting down on caffeine or limit how late you consume it
- cutting down on alcohol
- getting lighter blankets, or at least natural fibers like cotton (a friend of mine slept under a polyester bedspread—the artificial fibers trap the heat—with a partner and *three* dogs. She said to me, completely seriously, "I don't know why I keep waking up all sweaty; I guess I'm just a hot sleeper.")
- getting a weighted blanket

Some people hate weighted blankets, but in my personal and professional experience, a lot of people who thought they would hate them end up loving them. If you're thinking, "But Lara! You just said to make sure not to overheat," there are open-weave blankets that help solve that dilemma. The good-quality ones aren't cheap, but they're a great bargain compared to treating chronic health issues.

After you've tried everything else:
- get a sleep study for a CPap or BiPap if needed
- get your snoring partner to use one
- get an amicable "sleep divorce" and sleep separately

Some of these things may require a doctor's prescription or referral, but over the years, I've found that it's easier to get them than it used to be, probably because the need for sleep and the widespread problems people have with it are more recognized today than in the past decades. As for sleeping separately, I already know how unpopular this recommendation is for many of you. I promise, relationships and marriages actually get better, or at least have that potential, when both partners are rested and are not dealing with chronic irritability because they can't sleep. In my professional experience, couples who try this often report that it made their relationship better, not worse, as they feared.

I like to say to my grad students in clinical programs, "You are your instrument." Usually, this means you are your feelings, your history, your intuition, your perception—and you bring them to work with you every day. But your instrument is also your *body*. There are times that we human beings experience our bodies as a delight, as a burden, as an object for others to judge, or even a prison. For those of us who help, we also have to acknowledge it as our tool, whatever else we may feel about it, and artists take care of the instruments that allow them to practice their craft. We in these fields certainly are artists. Our instruments deserve our protection and our care.

CHAPTER THIRTEEN

The Rhino and the Unicorn: Starting Where You Really Are

"Even the smallest of creatures carries the sun in its eyes."
—Antonio Porchia, quoted in *The Angel and the Assassin*

In Herman's model, as with so many others that followed, reconnecting and integrating have to go beyond the self. As we have discussed reconnection to the body and the self, we now work to "rejoin the world". This could mean in our close relationships or finding our people out there in the world.

I've mostly talked about one part of joining the world that I think may be easy to miss: how we see ourselves, integrating a compassionate view of ourselves with our compassion for others. When we are constantly comparing ourselves to others, we make the world our enemy: always watching, always judging, never accepting. Learning to release this view doesn't just make it easier to be ourselves; it also makes it easier to imagine that other people see us gently, rather than harshly weighing our worth. When we value ourselves more, and we let go of the need to "please" others, we can be less afraid of them. And that makes it easier to connect.

One entry in the Rev. Nadia Bolz-Weber's blog called The Corners[153] has an illustration of a sweet, chubby rhino sweating away on a treadmill, gazing up at a poster of a unicorn on the wall. She writes about faith and about her life, and in this column, she tells us about her ongoing wish to be better, to be different. It's the same treadmill that I think most of us are on: the endless quest to achieve spiritual enlightenment, physical perfection, and the smooth, polished life that social media promises we can all have if we just keep trying (and subscribing and "liking," and on and on). Bolz-Weber writes, dryly funny as always, about her inevitable failure to be anything but herself. She says that somehow, God loves her and all the rest of us "madly," regardless (Bolz-Weber is a Lutheran pastor and speaks from a perspective of Christian faith, but substitute whatever you want here for that creative force that made you *you*, and not something else). She points out that her stubborn self-ness can heal and grow and learn—but she can't make herself into her ideal or into something she fundamentally is not. She can only ever be who she is, and that person will always be complicated, messy, and flawed.

I certainly relate to her words, but I think I respond mostly to the picture. No matter how long that rhino jogs along on the treadmill, it can't ever become a unicorn, for two very good reasons:

1. God did not make the rhino a unicorn; God made the rhino a rhino.

2. Unicorns aren't even real. *Nothing* can be a unicorn because they don't exist.

I kept thinking about this column months after I read it, and I realized that the gentle humor of the illustration nevertheless hit a spot of aching pain for me. The truth is that, like many of you, I have spent a lot of my life staring earnestly at the picture of whatever I believe is better, more beautiful, more accomplished, more valuable, more lovable than imperfect me. It hurts now to think of myself at age 11 or 12, just starting to learn from my peers, and from TV and magazine covers, that a unicorn, a creature that does not, cannot exist, was somehow better (and in fact, required) than the actual, shy, worried little rhino that *did* exist—the rhino that I was and still am. And I think the illustration did more than point out that pain. It also helped me to see that rhino more clearly: Adorable! Wearing a cute sweatband! Trying hard! Loveable and admirable for exactly what it is. Jogging on a treadmill is fine, but maybe while exercising, the rhino in the illustration would be better off with its *own* picture to gaze at on the wall, aiming to be nothing more or less than its own delightful rhino self.

Take Your Time

This understanding still comes and goes for me, and it's frustrating that I have to work on it even in what we're going to call *late middle age,* but I'm getting better at it as I get older. Getting better is enough, and I don't have to have some harsh, unattainable goal—even if it's the goal of letting go of unattainable goals! I can just keep jogging along and trust my sturdy rhino legs to carry me where I need to be. The pace really does not matter. There are many versions of this idea, but the first time I heard it, it was a Buddhist joke that went like this:

"If you improve only one percent in every lifetime, then in 100 lifetimes, you'll be the Buddha!" I loved this saying and started repeating it right away, because, as always, underneath the mild joke was some truth, and it was a comforting reprieve—improving a little over the course of one hundred lifetimes *is* fast enough, good enough. You don't have to flog yourself up the mountain, or into someone's heart, or God's grace. As Rick Fields, an American Buddhist leader, said, "The road to enlightenment is long and hard, and you should try not to forget to bring snacks and magazines."[154]

The idea of a gentle pace that you set for yourself helps me to unwind a tricky knot that always presents itself in these kinds of conversations: You have to love yourself first. When someone says this, a voice in my head always responds, *Ugh, really?* I have more gentleness and self-compassion than I used to, but I still get angry at myself regularly, and there have been times when hating myself was much closer than loving myself. As I said, I'm better at it now, but I still am not consistently great at loving myself all the time. Perhaps you aren't either. Maybe instead of setting yet another goal, we can try this idea on instead: Setting a hard goal (complete acceptance and self-love, in this case) sabotages the journey right from the start. So, let's not do that. Let's give everyone permission not to "love themselves first." How about "Try to be a little nicer to yourself today, and a little nicer than that tomorrow, and we'll see about the next day." It's not as concise and snappy, but I breathe a sigh of relief when I hear anyone, including myself, say something like this.

Another gift from Anne Lamott comes in her essay about her recovery from alcohol and drug abuse. She wrote that, little by little, her self-esteem improved from its previous state because, "It had been a while since I had consistently behaved in an estimable way."[155] I like this a lot. There is a difference between the vicious self-talk we sometimes use and the wildly unrealistic standards we set for ourselves that trigger it, versus acting like a person that we might like if we met them. In other words, if we start acting in ways that are not perfect, not Instagram-worthy or whatever, but that bring us satisfaction and self-respect, that's a good place to begin. In psychology, the term *self-efficacy* is as common as self-esteem, but you see it less in popular culture. They don't mean quite the same thing, but they relate closely to each other. In fact, self-esteem doesn't appear to be as powerful as self-efficacy. When you can do things that impact your environment—when you believe you can act in ways you want that will bring about the result you want—then you have a good sense of self-efficacy. You feel effective in the world. And that, of course, improves your opinion of yourself and bolsters your self-esteem. So, if I hold myself (gently, humorously) accountable and focus on setting goals I can follow through on, then I might be acting in a "consistently estimable way." I can feel effective in the world, in ways that I think are good or admirable. *Gently* is the key word here. There is a difference between holding ourselves accountable and holding ourselves hostage.

Maybe you have been doing things that are more serious than simply not heading toward your goals. Maybe you've been causing harm to yourself, either actively or through neglect. Maybe your actions have even hurt someone else. We are good at balancing a clear-eyed view of the damage or pain our clients have caused, while also seeing the damage and pain from which they act. We can be practical about what needs to change while steadfastly defending their humanity and their right to growth and redemption. We can do this for ourselves, too.

I also think Anne Lamott is pointing to something deeper still. Maybe, instead of starting with loving yourself, you need to heal yourself first to tolerate the vulnerability of loving yourself. Let me explain. One of the dilemmas in trauma healing is that when someone who has been hurt by other people experiences the holding and acceptance of the therapeutic relationship, they're torn because while one part of them has been craving this for a long time (maybe since they've been born), another part of them is absolutely terrified that letting down defenses will be a mistake, that they will be hurt and betrayed again by allowing help, especially if they have built safety around being self-reliant and alone. The therapist has to work hard to help the client through this, teaching their nervous system little by little that it's safe and OK to be cared for, and they aren't losing their ability to be strong or to protect themselves when needed, if they allow healthy support and acceptance into their lives.

If you have had these kinds of wounds, even loving *yourself* might be scarier than you can tolerate at times. After all, if you aren't constantly vigilant about your flaws and shortcomings, what if someone surprises you by attacking some failing you hadn't even noticed yet? You won't have armored yourself, either by removing or hiding the flaw first, or by beating yourself up about it so thoroughly that one more blow from someone else can't possibly hurt much more.

That reasoning looks absurd when you spell it all out, but I feel deep compassion for the need to protect ourselves in this way, especially if attacks or overly harsh criticism came without warning from an erratic, unpredictable person. In fact, unpredictability is one of the strongest reinforcements for behavior. If you can reliably predict when I'm going to be hurtful to you, then you have to be vigilant around me only at the times you know I'm likely to lash out. But if there isn't a pattern to my actions, or they come without warning, you need to be on guard against me *all the time*.

I once had a client tell me that when her grandmother surprised her once again with rage and verbal attacks after a period of relative calm, she would sit in her room and silently yell at herself. She wasn't directing her anger, even in her own head, at her grandmother for her inexcusable behavior, but at herself for letting her guard down and allowing herself to forget the danger and relax in her grandmother's company. When this kind of thing comes up in therapy, I am always firm about never being mad at a protective mechanism. I understood precisely why it was simply not safe enough, at that time, to hold her grandmother accountable for her actions. Scolding herself to shape up and stay more wary next time felt easier.

The problem with this strategy, as with so many of them, is that while it might make us *feel* safer, it's based on a lie. It's not really safety at all. We should be able to trust the people in our lives, and when they fail to act in a trustworthy way, we don't need to blame ourselves for expecting reasonable safety and caring from them. Yes, we have to set boundaries. Yes, we are ultimately responsible for who we let stay in our lives and what treatment we tolerate from them—if we are adults—but none of that means that we are more at fault than our abuser because our defensive vigilance wasn't enough to stop them.

This truth doesn't matter, though, if you were taught as a child, or in a relationship, that the only person who will prioritize your safety is you, and if you get hurt, it's your own fault. This lie may have been drilled in explicitly and deliberately by the person themselves; some abusers are very happy to tell you that their behavior is your fault. This can lead directly to mistaking fear or dread for guilt, as I mentioned earlier. Whether it's ever spelled out for us or not (and sometimes it is spelled out quite clearly), we may learn that it's our job to absorb and fix somebody else's uncomfortable feelings, and so we feel we really *have* done something wrong or failed if the other person still has those uncomfortable feelings that they take out on us. Even if we can see through this untruth at the time, it's hard to shake a feeling of complicity or responsibility: If we had done something, anything, differently, this wouldn't have happened. Thus, it's our job to keep it from happening, and constant monitoring and relentless self-criticism present themselves as the answer. It's a lesson that, once learned, runs deep. It takes time—sometimes a very long time—to unlearn this false lesson and allow gentleness, even from ourselves. So, before you get mad at yourself for failing to love yourself enough, maybe get help in healing and unlearning those lessons. That's how you can move forward in an honest and human way.

HAVE THE RIGHT TARGET

Like happiness, self-acceptance might best be aimed at indirectly, like the faint stars we can see only in our peripheral vision. If you look directly at them, they disappear; this is called "averted vision." The cones in the center of your eye aren't as sensitive as the rods at the edges, so you can catch a glimpse of the most distant stars only from the corner of your eye. I've talked elsewhere in this book about meaning and purpose. Positive psychology suggests that aiming to be "happy" in our lives may lead us to focus on the wrong things, like satiety. If you've ever noticed the up-and-down experience of highly anticipating something that is going to make you happy (a bowl of ice cream, a purchase, an accomplishment) and then that excitement quickly evaporates, it's not because you did it wrong. That happens because momentary enjoyment is, by definition, momentary. It won't last long, *and it was never meant to*. What we tend to do then is try to find just a little more of that initial feeling. It works again for a while, and then the cycle starts over.

When I was very young, I had a picture-book version of Disney's animated movie *Pinocchio*. The story didn't hold my interest much, except for the episode on Pleasure Island. Pleasure Island seriously freaked me out. On Pleasure Island, little boys got to do all the things that were usually forbidden. They smoked and played dice and got into fights, and they enjoyed these pastimes as much and as often as they wanted, with no consequences. *Or so it seemed.* Over time, they all sprouted the ears and tails of donkeys, having fallen victim to "Donkey Fever," and then the donkey-boys were put into harnesses and made to pull carts, weeping and wailing.[156] This scene utterly terrified me as a child, and I know now that this means that it did its job—it was supposed to scare me away from bad behavior, and it did.

But Pleasure Island also has a subtler lesson to teach, one that took me longer to understand. It points to the peril of having whatever you want, as much as you want, as often as you want it. Many cultures and religions quickly attribute this excess to sin, but we can keep it simple for our purposes: Too much of everything we want is simply not good for us and even makes us less ourselves over time. Given too much, for too long, may even cause us to lose some of our humanity. In other words, constant satiety is its own curse, and I think that in more everyday terms, the cycle of *wanting-getting let down-wanting* is evidence of this.

My point here is a small part of a larger argument, but it takes us where we need to be in this chapter—aiming at something more lasting, maybe just off to the side of what you're used to defining as "happiness," is the way to go. Meaning, purpose, being present in the moment as it is rather than trying to change it, are all ways that human beings feel lasting satisfaction rather than our fantasies of satiety.

Anne Lamott again offers a great way to sum this all up when she talked about her history of bingeing and purging food: "I was always starving, or stuffed, but never full."[157] So I'll pull these two Lamottian quotes together: Aiming to behave in a consistently estimable way (including speaking to yourself as kindly as you speak to everyone else) is a way of feeling full, not starving, or stuffed. We can feel safe in our own company. We can feed and nurture ourselves. And then we notice that having realistic expectations, modulated frustration or disappointment when we feel we've failed, and a gentle way of holding our vision of ourselves, gets a little easier. If this needs to be part of larger work on healing wounds, especially trauma-based self-reliance, that's OK. We might find that self-love can sneak its way in, after all.

If we aim directly at happiness, we tend to focus on pleasure and satiety, which is fleeting and ultimately a dead end. Aiming at meaning, connection, and purpose creates lasting gratification and deep peace. The chapter about Flow gives us some direction about what those aims might look like. And finally, we need to understand what we really want and can really receive from our aim. My childhood friend Edi Pasalis, a skilled and devoted Kripalu yoga practitioner and instructor for many years, leads a leadership and well-being coaching program focused on menopause.[158]

In a conversation several years ago about her yoga practice, she said, "I do yoga every day to learn about my real self." She never even mentioned cardio, or a "bikini body," or Instagram! How lovely, to aim at knowing and appreciating the self, rather than improving it. Who knows? Maybe this is the way that our self will finally be cherished by us.

JUST START

I'm not a professional organizer, as I've said earlier, or a behavior specialist, but I have observed what seems to help us humans make changes and what does not. One thing I feel passionately about is what you do not have to do. You don't have to go buy things, or clean out a room full of clutter, or reorganize your calendar first. In fact, put a little note in the mirror that you will do those things only if you are trying *not* to start—because those preconditions are the perfect way never to start anything, ever. Set up snazzy new equipment, shop for that fancy journal, remodel your garage into a gym *later*, when you're established and feel more confident about whatever it is you're trying to introduce into your life. Don't tell yourself that any of that has to happen until you're ready.

Next, do something before you feel like it, not the other way around. For so many things, from addiction to scrolling, we think that when we think and feel differently, we'll act differently. In fact, as a psychodynamic therapist who just loves to float around in meaning and feeling, I've had to grudgingly admit that this isn't really an efficient or effective way to make some kinds of changes in our lives.

Insight can and often does follow behavior change, but it rarely works the other way around. In other words, we learn something new about ourselves or the world *when we do something new*. Feelings can and often do shift after a challenge, like when we finally start that step goal we've been talking about. If we wait until our feelings are different (confident, excited, thrilled to be going out for a walk rather than dreading it), it will probably never happen. Doing something different will make you feel something different. So, start. I know this might be beyond cringey, but it's true—back when the Nike slogan "Just Do It" came out and was everywhere, it motivated me to start a modest exercise practice. I just . . . did it.

Something else you might well need to do before you feel totally ready to do it is set boundaries. If your life is consistently run over, it's hard to find the space for any of this. You really don't need that gorgeous home yoga studio setup, but you do need to be able to tell people to leave you alone for half an hour, turn off your phone, and then shut the door.

Luckily, this fits beautifully into the self-kindness conversation at the beginning of this chapter because boundaries, self-esteem/self-efficacy, and most of all self-compassion all fit hand in hand. Here are some ways we can set boundaries with ourselves first, as always.

I will not let anyone hurt, mistreat, or neglect this body—including me.

I will not let anyone talk cruelly to this person—including me.

I will not let anyone despise the universal human needs of this person (warmth, attention, safety, nourishment)—including me.

I will not let anyone squander the time I need to care for myself—including me.

I will not let anyone minimize or trivialize my right to rest and to heal—including and especially me.

IF YOU RUN OUT OF SELF-COMPASSION, BORROW SOME

If you're struggling to get out from under the weight of your own judgment and discouragement, it might help to ask someone who loves and cares about you about what they think about that endearing rhino on the treadmill of your life. This is usually not going to heal our deep wounds—we can only do that ourselves—but sometimes being seen and treated tenderly by another person can help remind us of how we should treat all humans, even ourselves. That momentary reminder might be enough to get us to put on a jacket and go for a walk, or take a minute alone to breathe, or find something good we did that day.

You, the smallest creature, carry the sun in your eyes. Maybe that can be enough.

The Sum of Light

"What then must we do?"

—"*Billy Kwan,*" *The Year of Living Dangerously*

At the beginning of this book, I told you about a conversation between two men confronting unbearable suffering, and the question that arose from it, "What then must we do?"

Here is what happens next: Billy answers his own question.

> You do what you can about the misery in front of you. *You add your light to the sum of light.*

And that is the best answer I have found in 30 years of asking myself this same question. I have no magical solutions to the problems of not enough time, not enough money, and too much pain. We do what we can, even when that seems atrociously, laughably unequal to the struggle. The Talmud answers Billy's question in a similar vein: You are not obligated to heal the world's grief. Neither are you free to abandon it.[159] Buddhism exhorts us not to turn away from the suffering of others. Catholics say the rosary; pilgrims walk the path of the Stations of the Cross. Every world religion tells us that pain is a fact of life and that we may not pretend otherwise, or ignore pain in others.

But to do this, to have light to add, we must keep our own flame lit. And that requires all the questioning, learning, self-reflection, and self-care I've illustrated throughout this book. There is a contradiction here, or maybe a better word is *paradox*. The paradox is in the fact that to do selfless work, we have to also focus on the self. There are a lot of paradoxes in this book, actually. To be able to be present, you might have to heal some injuries from the past. To accomplish more, you may need to learn to do less. To feel safe, you may need to let go of old ways that created a temporary illusion of safety, such as monitoring and people-pleasing. To feel more lasting happiness, you might need to aim at something else, like meaning or struggle.

As a therapist, I have learned that most of the human experience contains these paradoxes, and as I talked about in Chapter Four about defining what a problem is, we borrowed from the concept of Yin and Yang—two opposites that not only do not fight or try to vanquish the other, but serenely coexist, because neither one can be what it is without the contrast of the other. They are always shifting and moving, but they create perfect balance and wholeness that way. At any given moment, you might focus more on others, but you will inevitably need to tip the balance back toward yourself. This isn't failure, weakness, selfishness, or faltering in your commitment to helping— it's being in balance. It's how things are. It's how we are.

When we work to heal ourselves, and we've used Herman's stages of trauma healing as a framework for some of the ideas in this book, we find something to do in each stage. We have to find safety, reaching out for professional help for our pain or admitting that our efforts at numbing and distancing are starting to cause us real harm. Even when things aren't that dramatic, there still needs to be a safe place inside ourselves where we can say, *I am not doing OK. I need more of my own tenderness and care.*

Next, we have to mourn. We have to feel the pain of where we are. This is not the pain we already feel for our clients, some of whom are among the most vulnerable and the most alone. It's not the pain we try to ease in our loved ones, or whoever it is whose pain we're already carrying. We said in the introduction that some of that pain may need to be grieved, too, but this focus now is on you alone. We have to acknowledge and grieve *parts of ourselves* that feel lost in the struggle, or maybe some elements of our work that we have to change or release altogether. And finally, as we begin to feel safer and in less pain, we have to "rejoin the world," whether that means an actual community of people or simply to feel our place in a greater whole, one tiny, sparkling gleam on the waves. This brings us all the way back to light.

Remember the problem of light that we talked about in Chapter Four? Light cannot be *both* a particle *and* a wave, but it is. Whatever Grand Theory of Everything eventually adds all this up, we can be sure that the universe knew what it was doing all along. Light is effortlessly two "opposite" things at once. It doesn't worry about paradox. It *is* paradox. So, I've learned not to worry about paradox either. I can be as interested in my own well-being as the well-being of others, and these things can fit together. I can rest in the belief that I only have to do what is possible, what is in front of me in my little time here. That tiny effort cannot possibly affect all the suffering in the world in any mathematical, appreciable way—yet somehow, paradoxically, it is enough. I don't know yet—we humans don't know how both things can be true, but I still rest in the faith that they are.

You may take some strategies and tools from here, as well as craft your own. This will be an ongoing process and will evolve over time, as all organic things must. It is, if you are on the path of the helper, lifelong work to push back the dark.

As we've seen, sometimes we have been exposed to too much of that darkness. While I believe that helpers will *always* find ways to help (we have no choice, maybe), sometimes we have to attend to our own healing for a long time. We may need to leave our work and find something else entirely to do. My backup plan is working in a plant shop, but I think opening a dog bakery is also an excellent idea. If you open yours, I have no doubt you'll still want to connect and contribute to every soul that comes through the door for puppy biscuits, just like I'd no doubt find myself offering people comfort and advice when I'm supposed to be watering the azaleas.

If you need to leave your work as it is and find a place to rest, do it. You might worry that you have injuries too deep to heal, but remember, the human body does this all the time. We say that doctors and nurses heal people, but this is slightly inaccurate. Rather they mostly *remove barriers* to healing, like cleaning out the grit in a wound or giving antibiotics to combat an overrun of bacteria from infection. From there, the body employs its own intrinsic power and heals itself. A broken bone magically knits back together; an immune system repels the remaining invaders; a wound scabs over, and when the scab falls off, the skin beneath it is intact once more. There is often scar tissue left behind, yes, and sometimes a body will need a boost from the outside world, like medication or a prosthetic limb, but even so, our bodies are designed to *make themselves whole again.*

I believe this is true of psyche as well. We can remove our own barriers (often with help), and then healing, our natural state, kicks in again. Being human, you always have this capability. In Chapter Two, I quoted Donald Kalsched, depth psychologist and Jungian analyst, about what happens when our sense of self, of goodness, is damaged. He writes throughout his book about the way the deeper parts of us never really leave us, though trauma and disconnection can make them feel far away from us at times. He describes all the things he believes make up this true self, which he sums up as the soul, and I think that with or without religious connotations, this is the right word. Despite some of the almost unimaginable wounds his patients have sustained, he says, the soul remains. "When I speak of the soul in these pages [of his book], I will be referring to a vital animating core of our embodied selves; a certain *something* that links us (through love) to the divine, to each other, and to the exquisite beauties of the natural and cultural world. We know the soul when we experience it.[160]" There may be scars, and you may always need external support, just like some bodies do, but like your body, your psyche is designed to make itself whole. Give your soul what you need, allow your healing power what it requires, and remember that no human being is ever truly lost, no matter what we've seen, no matter what we've endured, no matter what we've done, or what we've failed to do. No matter what.

Canadian theologian Kate Bowler has written books and hosted podcasts about what it's like to be an internationally recognized thinker, bestselling author, happily married woman with a young son, and, since 2015, living with Stage 4 cancer and a terminal prognosis. She has this to say about confronting darkness, uncertainty, and pain:

> I have learned to live, and to love, without counting the cost; without reasons and assurances that nothing will be lost. Life will break your heart, and life may take everything you have and everything you hope for. But . . . I believe that in the darkness, even there, there will be beauty, and there will be love, and every now and then, it will feel like more than enough.

For me, this speaks right to the pain we helpers carry, fearing there will not be *enough:* not enough for our clients, not enough for the loved ones in our care, not enough for ourselves. Outrageously, Bowler suggests to us that even in the face of all we've struggled with, all the times we (or the systems we work for) have failed, we can move through our lives anyway. We can help anyway, stand in compassion and hope anyway, and, with all that we've seen and all that we've felt, even so, there will be times when it still feels like we have "more than enough."[161]

How can this be? How are we to act as helpers and carry that belief? A final word from Billy Kwan, our wise guide through the underworld: "We must give with love to whomever God places in front of us." I can do that for others and for myself as well. Training and skills and budgets all help, but when the things beyond my control threaten to make me despair, I remember that I can still meet with love whomever God (or what you like) places in front of me. That is always the choice I have, no matter what other resources are lacking.

I don't know if the world is better or worse than it was, or if that's even measurable, but I do know this: I, too, carry the sun in my eyes. My very being brings its own illumination. The world benefits from what I have to offer, however modest that is. When my own light shines, I can reflect that light back to others, and to myself as well, because I am worthy of my own attention. As time goes on, it sometimes seems that things are harder, or as a friend of mine said, "These days it seems like the good people are getting better, the bad people are getting worse, and the sick people are getting sicker." Maybe that's true, or maybe the world has always been this way—light and darkness, kind and heartless, held and free.[162] I don't know the answer. What I do know is that we need every single, shining one of you. Thank you for the bright beacon you are willing to offer this world. Thank you for your commitment to care for it and to keep it lit.

Thank you for the light you add to the sum of all our light.

The questions and exercises here are taken from various things we've talked about throughout the book. At the end of each section, there's space to write more, including anything that might relate to our tasks from Herman's stages of trauma healing: Safety and Stabilization; Mourning and Remembrance; and Reconnection and Integration.

Just like everything that has come before this, if anything feels too upsetting, intrusive, or uncomfortable, just skip it. Use what is helpful and discard anything that is not. Also, my commonsense warning to you is that *nothing here is diagnostic,* though some items have been derived from validated instruments such as the Moral Injury Symptom Scale-Healthcare Professionals. I've given you some items as snapshots only to help you reflect on any area that might need further attention. See a doctor or a licensed therapist to determine a diagnosis or a treatment plan. This book is a beginning, not the whole picture.

1. Secondary and Vicarious Trauma

This is not a validated instrument, just a compilation of experiences that we know from research can be linked with work stress, burnout, and secondary forms of trauma. This survey can give you an idea of how you're doing, not a way to diagnose yourself or anyone else. You can add up a score at the end to give you a sense of scale, but any item scored a three should get your attention.

Regardless of your score, if you are worried about anything on this list, take the time now to make an appointment to talk to someone.

Difficulty managing emotions

1. I feel like I'm a little edgy lately, but I'm not hearing about it from others.

2. I'm unusually moody, and people close to me have noticed.

3. I'm often volatile, angry and/or tearful, and people not close to me have noticed/remarked on it.

Feeling emotionally numb or shut down

1. I'm a little distracted lately, but I can focus when I want to.

2. I'm checking out more than usual, and it occasionally causes problems.

3. I'm very removed, and it's a repeated problem for me and/or people around me.

Difficulty falling asleep

1. I have some occasional issues falling or staying asleep, but it's OK.

2. Sleep is a regular problem, but I still get some good nights.

3. This happens nearly every night.

Fatigue or sleepiness during the day

1. I need a little more effort to get through the day right now.

2. I often struggle to stay awake and/or alert.

3. Getting through each day is hard.

Physical problems or complaints, such as aches, pains, and decreased resistance to illness

1. I've noticed this lately, but my health is basically the same.

2. I'm getting minor illnesses (colds, etc.) more frequently, or my usual health issues are a little worse.

3. I have a new, serious sickness or pain, or my usual health issues are much worse.

Relationship problems (e.g., withdrawing from friends and family, increased interpersonal conflicts, avoiding intimacy)

1. I'm not connecting as much as usual for me, but I'm still seeing and talking to people.
2. I've been avoiding things, and people occasionally point it out to me.
3. This has become a major problem for the people in my life.

Lack of or decreased participation in activities that used to be enjoyable

1. I haven't gotten to do fun things lately, but they're next on my list!
2. I'm struggling to connect to fun things.
3. I have no interest in doing any of the fun things I used to do, and I don't have new ones in mind.

Avoiding work and interactions with clients or constituents

1. Sometimes I daydream about taking a day off to avoid things, but I rarely do.
2. I have taken a sick/personal day recently, and it was at least partly avoidance.
3. I am missing or late to work regularly or doing other things to avoid stressful work.

Destructive coping or addictive behaviors (e.g., over/under-eating, substance abuse, gambling, taking undue risks in sports or driving)

1. I've been over-indulging in these things occasionally, but it's generally not an issue.

2. I am increasingly doing things that are concerning to me and/or to the people close to me.

3. I am in trouble.

Negative self-image

1. After a tough day, I question my abilities, but I usually know I'm doing OK.

2. I've noticed more days when I feel bad/guilt/shame, especially connected to work.

3. I regularly feel intense shame, guilt, self-doubt, or inadequacy related to my work.

Reduced ability to feel sympathy and empathy (can include "jumping ahead" rather than hearing a story, or unfairly comparing their suffering to others' that seems worse)

1. I sometimes find ways to jump ahead mentally in a story or minimize someone's pain, but I catch it and correct myself without people being aware of it.

2. I have jumped ahead or minimized enough that I've been called out on it, or it caused someone to notice my lack of connection.

3. I am struggling to listen or care, and this has caused me to be reprimanded or deliver subpar care to clients.

Scoring

Low (1-11) May indicate mild or occasional problems with secondary traumas or empathetic injury

Moderate (12-22) May indicate a moderate or increasing problem with secondary traumas or empathetic injury

High (23-33) May indicate a significant problem with secondary traumas or empathetic injury.

If you have scored in the High range (23 or above) or you have scored a three in any category, please take this seriously and check in with a doctor or therapist.

Here are some additional items from Gentry and Dietz's cross-walked PTSD/vicarious trauma symptoms:

Intrusion

- Having frequent dreams or nightmares about work
- Becoming preoccupied with particular patients or clients
- Letting patient/work issues encroach on your personal time
- Seeing yourself as a "savior," the only one who knows how to properly care for others
- Feeling a sense of entitlement that causes you to flout rules or ignore conventions
- Constantly thinking and feeling inadequate about your role as a care provider
- Categorizing everyone as either a potential victim or a potential perpetrator
- Perceiving the world as increasingly dangerous

Avoidance

- Tuning out clients when they tell you about their traumatic experiences
- Losing interest in activities you once enjoyed or abandoning self-care activities
- Pervasive feelings of fatigue or hopelessness
- Dreading routine tasks or the prospect of working with particular patients
- Losing confidence in your competence/effectiveness as a caregiver

- Withdrawing from friends and family to spend long hours engaging in escapist pursuits such as watching television or online gaming
- Using alcohol, drugs, sex, food, shopping, or other self-soothing strategies to ward off feelings of fear, anxiety, or depression
- Increased conflicts with loved ones who express worries about your behavior

Negative alterations in cognition and mood
- Feelings of detachment or estrangement from colleagues and patients
- Feeling cynical or hopeless about your caregiving career
- Inability to draw pleasure or satisfaction from caregiving successes and inordinate concern with perceived caregiving failures
- Distorted perception of yourself as either inadequate or superior
- Blaming patients and colleagues for poor outcomes
- Difficulty summoning the energy needed to fulfill caregiving responsibilities.
- Abandoning relationships or interests that once sustained you
- Disorganization, clutter, and procrastination [my addition]

If you have any current thoughts of self-harm or suicide or harming somebody else, *please stop what you are doing* and call the Suicide Hotline at 988 in the USA or check the hotline in your region or country.

NOTES

The Trauma around You

How often do you hear identified/diagnosed trauma narratives at work?

____

How often do you hear/read about identified/diagnosed trauma narratives in your personal life?

____

How often do you hear/read about unidentified/spontaneous trauma narratives at work?

____

How often do you hear/read about unidentified or spontaneous trauma narratives in your personal life?

____

How often do people enact traumatic dysregulation around you without acknowledgment of the trauma?

____

Do you have professional training, supervision, and support for this?

____

Is It Stress or Is It Trauma?

In _The Myth of Normal_, Maté distinguishes between normal stress and stress that can become overwhelming and/or traumatic. When you reflect on your stress, particularly the stress related to your work, how would you answer the following?

Does the stress you feel limit you, constrict you, diminish your capacity to think or feel or trust or assert yourself, or to experience suffering without succumbing to despair?

Yes   No

Can you witness suffering with compassion?

Yes   No

Does your stress keep you from holding your pain and sorrow and fear without being overwhelmed and without having to escape habitually into work or compulsive self-soothing or self-stimulating by whatever means?

Yes   No

Are you left compelled either to aggrandize yourself or to efface yourself for the sake of gaining acceptance, or to justify your existence?

Yes   No

Does your stress impair your capacity to experience gratitude for the beauty and wonder of life?

Yes   No

1. Moral Injury

These items are taken from the Moral Injury Symptom Scale—Healthcare Professionals. (MISS-HP). The outline I've included here is not scored; to get a valid scored assessment, you should work with a mental health or healthcare professional who can administer and interpret it. This is just to give you a sense of what moral injury can look like and help you decide if you do want to have an assessment.

- betrayal
- moral concerns
- loss of trust
- loss of meaning
- unforgiveness
- self-condemnation
- feeling punished by God
- loss of religious faith

What are mistakes (things *in your control*) that you can avoid when acting as a good and moral helper?

____

What are barriers (things *outside of your control*) to acting as a good and moral helper?

____

What can you do to hold yourself in compassion for those mistakes or barriers?

____

When do you need to renew your belief in yourself as a good and moral person?

____

What values are important to you as a good and moral person?

____

Here is my Code of Honor (based on these values):

____

____

____

What are the people, places, and things that help support and remind you of this code/values?

____

2. Compassionate Empathy

What are the signals that you are in a state of emotional empathy and being merged/overwhelmed with the emotions of the other person?

sensations ____________________________________

feelings ______________________________________

thoughts ______________________________________

What are the signals that you are in a state of compassionate empathy, aware of your own well-being while holding compassion for the other person?

sensations ____________________________________

feelings ______________________________________

thoughts ______________________________________

What are the situations most likely to require you to move from emotional empathy to compassionate empathy?

____

What do you do to move into compassionate empathy?

____

Exercise: Loving-kindness meditation (note: substitute with another meditation if desired)

When and where you will do this: _______________________

Who you will picture: _______________________

What you try to notice after you are done: _______________________

How often would you like to be practicing this: _______________________

3. Changing What a Problem Is

What are some problems in your life that you can solve "permanently" (end a relationship, etc.)

____

What are some problems of living you will encounter again and again?

____

What can you tell your future self for when those problems return, either in their old form or a new one?

____

What does it look like when you are being strong like an oak?

____

What does it look like when you are being strong like a willow?

____

What lets you know which type of strength you might want to use, or when it's time to switch from one to the other?

____

4. Tolerating Strong Emotions

Exercise: Wings of the Bird

What emotion are you noticing right now, and where can you touch in with it the most directly in your body?

____

What word or phrase best describes the sensation? (You can think about texture, size, temperature, color, intensity, or any other sense that comes to you)

____

What emotion word or phrase connects best with it? (It may have changed since you started the exercise)

____

Ask in whatever version fits best for you this question: Can you:

a. give permission for that sensation and emotion to be here just for right now?

b. make space in your body for that sensation and emotion just for right now?

c. Say "yes" to that sensation and emotion that is happening just for right now?

How often would you like to practice this? _______________________

Healing Task: For Safety and Stabilization, is there anything that needs to be addressed right away so that you can stay safe, have a crisis plan, or make your environment more stable? Is there anything not mentioned in these questions that you'd like to add?

____

5. Intuition and Messages from Your True Self

What signals let you know something inside you is trying to get your attention (jokes, dreams, intuition)?

____

What signals are easy to listen to, and what signals are harder or make you want to ignore them?

____

What signals or themes do you see popping up frequently in the world around you? (This could be repeated phrases, things friends have said, or things in nature that keep getting your attention).

____

How does your shadow get your attention?

____

What parts of your shadow do you find hardest to acknowledge, and what helps to do this?

____

Have you gotten a signal from yourself that you might need to make changes in your life?

____

If so, what resources or help do you have in order to make that change?

____

If you cannot make the changes you need in your work or life now, what is the next step you can take to do something else entirely?

____

6. Regulation in the Moment

What are three strategies you can use *in the moment* to physically regulate yourself?

____

____

____

7. Regulation over Time

What are three practices or routines you can use over time, whether daily, weekly, or monthly, that help you to feel grounded, present, and regulated?

____

____

____

8. Distraction and Flow

How do you recognize or notice the differences between Distraction and Flow states?

____

What are the conditions and situations most likely to make you vulnerable to bingeing or numbing out?

____

What are three things you can do to gently get yourself out of a numbed binge state?

____

____

____

What are three activities you can start *right now* (in other words, you don't need to buy expensive equipment or take classes) to create a Flow state for you?

____

____

____

For different neurochemicals, try different things: As always, this is not a substitute for medical advice, and these examples are simple ways to describe complex chemical interactions. Try what works for you and talk with a professional before starting anything new, like rigorous exercise or adjusting your diet. I DO NOT recommend supplements claiming to "boost" anything on this list, as this tends toward a lot of pseudoscience, some of which can be dangerous. Nothing here or on the Internet replaces talking with your doctor.

Dopamine: something that gives sensory pleasure; a quick reward like checking off a task or winning a game

____

Serotonin: sustained effort and accomplishment; time in nature, mindfulness practice, sunlight

____

Endorphins: chocolate! (dark is best; may also release cannabinoids and repel Dementors); vigorous exercise/cardio, laughing, spicy food

---

Oxytocin and/or vasopressin: physical touch, sex, cuddling, petting an animal, hugging your child

---

GABA: yoga, meditation, Tai Chi, sunlight

Healing Task: When you practice regulation in the moment or over time, are there sensations, feelings, or memories that come up and ask for your attention? Is there anything that your true self is trying to tell you that you need to remember, feel, or mourn? If so, can you give them space and attention, or does it feel too overwhelming to allow this? If so, this might be something that can be supported in therapy.

---

9. Daily Rituals

These may include formal religious practices, but they can also be personal, simple actions with no religious significance. Naturally, you can have both in your life if you want!

What is a *liminal ritual* you can use to let yourself know you are done with your work/responsibilities for the day or are shifting from one "world" to another?

What is a *cleansing ritual* you can use to let yourself know that whatever is burdensome or troubling from your day has been washed away, cleared, or released?

____

What is a *transcending ritual* that you can use to let yourself feel connected or "plugged in" to something bigger than you? (This can be nature, God, the universe, divine help, etc., whatever is most meaningful to you.)

____

What is a *communion ritual* that you can use to let yourself feel a part of the people in your life? (This could include gathering for a meal, saying a simple grace, connecting to people for special time like volunteering or a shared interest.)

____

Healing Task: How does it feel to begin reconnecting to the world? If it feels approachable, using the steps you've worked on is a great start! If it still feels like too much and makes you want to retreat, you may need more time to remember, mourn, or process with someone in therapy. Which feels true for you right now?

____

____

____

____

10. Making a Beginning

What is your "one thing" where you're going to start to change how you take care of yourself? You can have more than one thing, taking something from each section of the book, or you can choose *just one thing,* and come back at any time to choose the next one:

____

What are the barriers to doing this?

____

How will you get around them?

____

Who can help you prioritize this?

____

As you approach the end of these steps, do you feel that you rushed through anything and you'd like more time with it? It's OK to go back and spend more time with anything in this book! Is there anything you skipped that you'd like to come back to another time? It's OK to make a plan to do your other healing work first.

This process is a spiral; you could go through each step over and over. If it's a helpful process for you, you'll feel and observe different things each time. Mostly, this is the time to ask yourself if you feel ready to continue reconnecting to yourself, your work, and your world, or if you need more time, more support, or more help. Whatever is right for you is the right answer.

In some ways, spending years thinking about and then writing a book can be weirdly isolating, as if you live for a while on a tiny planet, all by yourself. The truth is that nothing would have come of any of it without a lot of other people. Let me give a few examples here:

The National Association for the Dually Diagnosed (NADD)—particularly Jeanne Farr and Carly Winnie—allowed this all to happen in the first place. I so appreciate your leadership and support.

The distinguished Dr. Susan Havercamp reviewed this manuscript, as did the multi-talented Dr. Karsten Look and the luminous Dr. Janice Glowski. Wise friends all. I'm lucky to know you.

The Superfriends editing and design team made this book work. Led by the amazing (and indefatigable) Jennifer Scroggins, designer Mark Sullivan brought his unfailing good taste, while Jennifer, Kathleen Carroll, and Richelle Thompson caught everything that was bad but could be fixed and everything that was okay but could be better.

Dr. Bruce Davis took time from working on his book to write the foreword to mine, which was characteristically generous of him.

Kevin Aldridge provided research, expertise, and advice—oh, and kept our business running.

My father, stepmother, and brother offered advice, support, and encouragement, and my sister's beautiful art installation provided the imagery that opens Chapter Six.

Edi Pasalis, childhood friend and fellow Ruffing Montessori alumna, kindly contributed her insight about yoga. She is a lovely and smart human being, and you should check out her website.

My students were an early and discerning audience, as well as cheerful ~~guinea pigs~~ collaborators on some of this material. Our

Aldridge Palay clients and partners helped me to develop and hone even more of it.

My clinical clients, past and present, have done me the profound honor of letting me be a part of their work to heal and grow.

Finally, and most of all, my husband, Darren Thompson, helped me to see what this book is really about.

To all of you—I'm gratefully in your debt.

Alberti, R. E., & Emmons, M. L. (2017). *Your perfect right: Assertiveness and equality in your life and relationships* (10th ed.). Impact Publishers.

Barrett, L. F. (2017). *How emotions are made: The secret life of the brain.* Mariner Books.

Blackburn, E. H., & Epel, E. S. (2017). *The telomere effect: A revolutionary approach to living younger, healthier, longer.* Grand Central Publishing.

Bolz-Weber, N. (2013). *Pastrix: The cranky, beautiful faith of a sinner & saint.* Jericho Books.

Brach, T. (2003). *Radical acceptance: Embracing your life with the heart of a Buddha.* Bantam.

Brach, T. (2019). *Radical compassion: Learning to love yourself and your world with the practice of RAIN.* Viking.

Chödrön, P. (2001). *Comfortable with uncertainty: 108 teachings on cultivating fearlessness and compassion.* Shambhala Publications.

Chödrön, P. (2002). *The places that scare you: A guide to fearlessness in difficult times.* Shambhala Publications.

Cope, S. (1999). *Yoga and the quest for the true self.* Bantam.

de Becker, G. (1997). *The gift of fear and other survival signals that protect us from violence.* Dell Publishing.

Eliade, M. (1959). *The sacred and the profane: The nature of religion* (W. R. Trask, Trans.). Harcourt Brace.

Epstein, M. (2014). *The trauma of everyday life.* Penguin Books.

Evans, W., Walser, R. D., & Hayes, S. C. (2020). *The moral injury workbook: Acceptance and commitment therapy skills for moving beyond shame, anger, and trauma to reclaim your values.* New Harbinger Publications.

Gentry, J. E., & Dietz, J. (2020). *Forward-facing Professional resilience: Prevention and resolution of burnout, toxic stress and compassion fatigue.* Routledge.

Hyde, L. (1998). *Trickster makes this world: Mischief, myth, and art.* Farrar, Straus and Giroux.

Nakazawa, D. J. (2020). *The angel and the assassin: The tiny brain cell that changed the course of medicine.* Ballantine Books.

Kalsched, D. (2013). *Trauma and the soul: A psycho-spiritual approach to human development and its interruption.* Routledge.

Khoudari, L. (2021). *Lifting heavy things: Healing trauma one rep at a time.* Penguin Life.

Lindenfeld, G. (2015). *First responders: Compassion fatigue, burnout, PTSD.* CreateSpace Independent Publishing Platform.

Maté, G. (2003). *When the body says no: Exploring the stress–disease connection.* Wiley.

Maté, G., & Maté, D. (2022). *The myth of normal: Trauma, illness, and healing in a toxic culture.* Avery.

Palay, L. (2021). *The way through: Trauma responsive care for developmental disability professionals.* NADD.

Papadopoulos, R. K. (Ed.). (2020). *Moral injury and beyond: Understanding human anguish and healing traumatic wounds.* Routledge.

Price, U., & Baker, D. J. (2023). *The good stuff: Practical positive supports for people with intellectual and developmental disabilities and mental illness.* NADD Press.

Sawicki, S. (2019). Mental health work's vicarious trauma, secondary traumatic stress, and self-care. [Independently published doctoral dissertation, University of Virginia].

Stone, A. (2012). *Fooling Houdini: Magicians, mentalists, math geeks, and the hidden powers of the mind.* HarperCollins.

Tawwab, N. G. (2021). *Set boundaries, find peace: A guide to reclaiming yourself.* Tarcher.

Tzu, L. (ca. 400 BCE). *Tao Te Ching.*

1. Weir, P. (Director). (1982). *The year of living dangerously* [Film]. Metro-Goldwyn-Mayer.

2. Luke 3:10, NKJV.

3. I'm paraphrasing here what I think is the most tragically beautiful sentence in Lincoln's speeches, from his second inaugural address, 1865.

4. Maté, G., & Maté, D. (2022). *The myth of normal: Trauma, illness and healing in a toxic culture.* Avery.

5. Ibid.

6. Ibid.

7. Herman, J. (1992) *Trauma and Recovery.* Basic Books.

8. King, S. (1980). *Danse Macabre.* Everest House.

9. Canada Border Services Agency—Pacific Region. (2006). *Critical incident stress management (CISM) program, Canada Border Services Agency—Pacific Region: CISM mass event response plan 2006.*

10. Mathieu, F. (2012). *The compassion fatigue workbook.* Routledge.

11. This is a completely hypothetical example.

12. Maté and Maté. (2022). *The myth of normal: Trauma, illness and healing in a toxic culture.* Avery.

13. Woodhead, E., et al. (2016). Stress, social support, and burnout among long-term care nursing staff. *Journal of Applied Gerontology.*

14. Kanios, A., & Bocheńska-Brandt, A. (2021). Occupational burnout among workers in the long-term care sector in relation to their personality traits. *International Journal of Occupational Medicine and Environmental Health. 34(4):491-504.*

15. Nazir, A., et al. (2018). The prevalence of burnout among nursing home physicians: An international perspective. *Journal of the American Medical Directors Association. Jan;19(1) 86-88.*

16. Dutheil, F., et al. (2019). Suicide among physicians and health-care workers: A systematic review and meta-analysis. *PloS one, 14*(12), e0226361. https://doi.org/10.1371/journal.pone.0226361

17. Maggu, G., Dhamija, S., Chaudhury, S., Rohatgi, S., Saldanha, D., & Jain, S. (2021). Behavioral presentations of focal onset seizures: A case series. *Industrial Psychiatry Journal, 30*(Suppl 1), S204–S209. https://doi.org/10.4103/0972-6748.328869

18. National Child Traumatic Stress Network.

19. Pearlman, L. A. & Caringi, J. C. (2009). Vicarious traumatization and complex trauma. In C. A. Courtois & J. D. Ford (Eds.), *Complex traumatic stress disorders: An evidence-based clinician's guide* (pp. 202-224). Guilford Press.

20. Sawicki, S. (2019). Mental health work's vicarious trauma, secondary traumatic stress, and self-care. [Independently published doctoral dissertation, University of Virginia].

21. Gentry, J. E., & Dietz, J. L. (2020). *Forward-facing professional resilience: Prevention and resolution of burnout, toxic stress, and compassion fatigue.* Outskirts Press.

22. When I worked as a sexual abuse investigator in child protective services, I noticed this effect almost immediately. I could not go to a restaurant without thinking I could "identify" the kids who were being harmed and adults who were likely to be harming them, just by looking. They seemed to be *everywhere*. In retrospect, while I believe my intuition is generally strong, my "vibes" in those moments were probably a reaction to the shocking, overwhelming world I'd been plunged into rather than any valid perception on my part. In other words, though I may have been right in some cases, even the high rates of abuse wouldn't have matched how often I thought I was seeing it.

23. Chou, C., et al. (2018). How is hoarding related to trauma? A detailed examination on different aspects of hoarding and age when hoarding started. *Journal of Obsessive-Compulsive and Related Disorders.* Vol. 16, Pages 81–87, ISSN 2211-3649. The relationship between ACEs, adult trauma, and issues of disorganization is not well understood and a matter of some academic debate, but there is a demonstrable link reported between more severe forms of clutter issues such as hoarding and trauma, as the study above discusses. Anecdotally, many of my trauma clients report serious struggles with clutter, disorganization, and procrastination. We'll see what research develops in this area.

24. Levine, P. A. (2022). Foreword. In G. Maté & D. Maté, *The myth of normal: Trauma, illness, and healing in a toxic culture* (pp. x–xii). Avery.

25. Ibid.

26. https://ww.findagrave.com/memorial/246048914/eugene-marion-simmers.

27. VanderWeele, T. J., Wortham, J. S., Carey, L. B., Case, B. W., Cowden, R. G., Duffee, C., Jackson-Meyer, K., Lu, F., Mattson, S. A., Padgett, R. N., Peteet, J. R., Rutledge, J., Symons, X., & Koenig, H. G. (2025). Moral trauma, moral distress, moral injury, and moral injury disorder: definitions and assessments. *Frontiers in psychology, 16*, 1422441. https://doi.org/10.3389/fpsyg.2025.1422441. See also: Birch, M. J., Inhaber, J., & Ashbaugh, A. R. (2024). Morally uncertain: the influence of intolerance of uncertainty and perceived responsibility on moral pain. *Anxiety, Stress, & Coping, 38*(4), 423–435. https://doi.org/10.1080/10615806.2024.2423436

28. Useless at doing the job of any proper medical mask. Not getting into a facemask debate here.

29. Shay, J. (1994). *Achilles in Vietnam: Combat trauma and the undoing of character*. Scribner.

30. Z Dogg.

31. Shay, J. (1994). *Achilles in Vietnam: Combat trauma and the undoing of character*. Scribner.

32. As I was working on the final drafts of this book, a nurse in a Columbus hospital was allegedly strangled by a hospital visitor when she tried to intervene in a conflict between him and a patient. The nurse was trying to protect the infant the man was holding at the time. Charges have been filed and the case is pending. The president of the Ohio Nurses Association described this as "a troubling example of a persisting national problem." November 9, 2025, NBC4i.com; updated November 11, 2025. Retrieved 12/1/25.

33. Ibid.

34. Ibid.

35. Davis, K. L., & Montag, C. (2019). Selected Principles of Pankseppian Affective Neuroscience. *Frontiers in neuroscience, 12*, 1025. https://doi.org/10.3389/fnins.2018.01025. Jaak Panskepp identified the neural

"circuits" identified with primary, survival-based affective functions in our brains, including SEEKING, CARE, PLAY, and LUST, which he described as positive, and RAGE, FEAR, and SADNESS as the negative.

36. Mitchell, D., & Webb, R. (Writers and Performers). (2005, February 10). *That Mitchell and Webb sound*, Series 2, Episode 1 [Radio broadcast]. BBC Radio 4, London, England.

37. Maté, G. and Maté, D. (2022). *The myth of normal: Trauma, illness and healing in a toxic culture.* Avery.

38. Shay, J. (1994). *Achilles in Vietnam: combat trauma and the undoing of character.* Scribner.

39. Gemmill, R. S., Wells, J., & Wyle, N. (Executive Producers). (2025–present). *The Pitt* [TV series]. John Wells Productions; Warner Bros. Television. https://www.hbomax.com/shows/pitt-2024/e6e7bad9-d48d-4434-b334-7c651ffc4bdf. We will all be processing the pandemic for years to come, but some in the medical and first responder world will be processing it forever.

40. To be extremely clear: I was supporting a recommendation he'd already gotten from his doctor, not prescribing or even suggesting a specific medication, which would be outside the scope of my license. But it's worth noting that he had to go to a different city even to talk to a physician for himself, to be sufficiently comfortable that no one would know. I didn't think he was exhibiting paranoia because he had no other symptoms or indicators of psychosis, so I had to conclude that he had some reasonable grounds for his worry. Other medical professionals I've seen since have echoed his fears.

41. Shay, J. (1994). *Achilles in Vietnam: Combat trauma and the undoing of character.* Scribner.

42. Ibid.

43. Van der Kolk, B. (2015). *The body keeps the score: Brain, mind and body in the healing of trauma.* Penguin Books.

44. Kalsched, D. (2013). *Trauma and the soul: A psycho-spiritual approach to human development and its interruption.* Routledge.

45. Mantri, S., Lawson, J., & Wang, Z. Identifying moral injury in healthcare professionals: The Moral Injury Symptom Scale-HP. *Journal of Religion and Health.* Oct; 59 (5): 2323-2340.

46. Brock, R. (2020). Moral injury. In R. Papadopoulos (Ed.). *Moral injury and beyond: Understanding human anguish and healing traumatic wounds.* Routledge.

47. Current Archaeology. (2013). Time heals: Digging Caerwent with Operation Nightingale. *Current Archaeology.* https://www.archaeology.co.uk. Retrieved 9/14/25.

48. Gentry, J., and Dietz, J. (2020). *Forward Facing Professional Resilience: Prevention and Resolution of Burnout, Toxic Stress and Compassion Fatigue.* Outskirts Press.

49. Evans, T., et al. (2020). *The moral injury workbook: Acceptance and commitment skills for moving beyond shame, anger, and trauma to reclaim your values.* New Harbinger Publications. This workbook takes a comprehensive ACT approach to moral injury, more than I can reproduce here, and I recommend it highly.

50. Shay, J. (1994). *Achilles in Vietnam: Combat trauma and the undoing of character.* Scribner.

51. Kalsched, D. (2013). *Trauma and the soul: A psycho-spiritual approach to human development and its interruption.* Routledge.

52. Singer, T., & Klimecki, O. M. (2014). Empathy and compassion. *Current Biology, 24*(18), R875–R878. https://doi.org/10.1016/j.cub.2014.06.054

53. Aldridge, K. (Anticipated 2026). *Keeping the lights on: organizational strategies and tools for burnout* (working title). NADD Press.

54. World Health Organization, updated 2019. https://www.who.int/news/item/28-05-2019-burn-out-an-occupational-phenomenon-international-classification-of-diseases. Retrieved September 2025.

55. Maslach, C. (1982). *Burnout: The cost of caring.* Prentice-Hall.

56. Maté, G. and Maté, D. (2022). *The myth of normal: Trauma, illness and healing in a toxic culture.* Avery.

57. Klimecky, O. M., & Singer, T. (2011). Empathic distress rather than compassion fatigue? Integrating findings from empathy research in psychology and social neuroscience. In B. Oakley, A. Knafo, G. Madhavan, & D. S. Wilson (Eds.), *Pathological altruism* (pp. 368-384). Oxford University Press.

58. Singer, T. and Klimecki, O. M. (2014). Brain regions involved in empathy and compassion. *Current Biology, 24*(18), R876–R878. https://doi.org/10.1016/j.cub.2014.06.054

59. Be sure to share this little tidbit with any medical folks among your friends and family—they'll love it.

60. Dr. Tania Singer at the Max Planck Institute and Dr. Simon Baron-Cohen at Cambridge are two of the more recognizable names in the neurology of empathy, a field with arguably hundreds of researchers and new studies being published all the time.

61. Ogden, P. (2021). The way through. In L. Palay (Ed.), *Trauma responsive care for intellectual and developmental disabilities professionals* (p.13). NADD Press.

62. Did you know that when squirrels lie flat on the railing of your porch or on the sidewalk to cool off, there's a term for it? It's called *splooting*, and despite our tense standoff in the Battle for the Deck, I admit that it's pretty adorable when they do that.

63. Don't worry, I'm not going down without a fight.

64. The Focus Project. (2025, April). *Bearing witness: Death-camp liberators and Holocaust survivors*. Jewish News Service. https://www.jns.org

65. Porges, S. (2021). The Polyvagal theory: Neurophysiological foundations of emotions, attachment, communication and self-regulation. Norton. In L. Palay (Ed.), *The way through: Trauma responsive care for intellectual and developmental disabilities professionals* (pp. 46; 52). NADD Press.

66. Singer, T. and Klimecki, O. M. (2014). Brain regions involved in empathy and compassion. *Current Biology, 24*(18), R876–R878. https://doi.org/10.1016/j.cub.2014.06.054

67. Groves, R., & Klausner, H. (2009). *The American book of living and dying*. Clarkson Potter/Ten Speed.

68. Hebrews 11:1, NKJV.

69. Singer, B. (Director). (2003). *X2: X-Men United [Film]*. 20th Century Fox; Marvel Enterprises; Bad Robot.

70. Przyrembek, M., et al. (2019). Loving-kindness meditation — A queen of hearts? *Journal of Consciousness Studies, 26* (7–8), S. 95–129.

71. My thanks to Dr. Glowski and the Columbus Shambhala Center.

72. Łoś, K., Łuczyński, W., & Waszkiewicz, N. (2022). Can the practice of mindfulness reduce medical errors? *Postepy psychiatrii neurologii*, 31(3), 121–127.

73. Lee, R., et al. (2018). *Integrative body mind spirit social work: An empirically based approach to assessment and treatment* (Vol. 2). Oxford University Press.

74. Sorry, Ohio State.

75. Lee, R., et al. (2018). *Integrative body mind spirit social work: An empirically based approach to assessment and treatment* (Vol. 2). Oxford University Press.

76. It was the nineties; we were very granola. For the record, I would *not* do that again, but some people love it.

77. Brach, T. (2004). *Radical acceptance: Embracing your life with the heart of a Buddha*. Bantam. I have condensed and summarized this exercise, which you can find in her many writings and interviews, including her subsequent book *Radical Compassion*.

78. Palay, X. (1994). *Graffiti of the spirit world*. Art installation, Columbus, Ohio.

79. Poehler, A. (2014). *Yes Please*. Dey Street, New York. The obsession with *The Gift of Fear* is just one of the many things Amy and I have in common. Actually, it's not so much "many things" and more like two things: We both love that book and recommend it constantly, and we both are short and do not like to be picked up off the ground. That's it, really.

80. de Becker, G. (1998). *The gift of fear*. Dell.

81. Any therapist will tell you—we are always our own WORST, MOST STUBBORN client.

82. Storr, A. (2014). *The essential Jung*. Princeton University Press.

83. Kevin, with his philosophy master's, would like me to point out that it was Aristotle.

84. Chen, A. (2018). How accurate are personality tests? *Scientific American*. https://www.scientificamerican.com/article/how-accurate-are-personality-tests/

85. OCEAN Big Five was developed by Lewis Goldberg in 1993, based on earlier work by Tupes, Fiske, and others.

86. Storr, A. (2014). *The essential Jung*. Princeton University Press.

87. Yes, I know wolves aren't likely to do this—this is a tale we're telling, so this is a fairy tale wolf. Very appropriate for Jung.

88. Ibid.

89. Matthew 7:3. "And why do you look at the speck in your brother's eye, but do not consider the plank in your own eye?" NKJV.

90. The other two commandments are: Feelings are value-neutral, and feelings are temporary.

91. Hassan, S. (2015) *Combating cult mind control*. Park Street Press.

92. Ibid.

93. FLDS stands for Fundamentalist Church of Jesus Christ of Latter-Day Saints. They call themselves Mormons, but the Mormon Church does not recognize them. In 1904, the Mormon Church renounced polygamy and in the 1930s formally excommunicated its members who maintained polygamy, which is the whole deal with the FLDS. They're a well-recognized and studied cult, and their current leader is in prison for life for child sexual assault and child rape. The organization itself has been charged with multiple serious offenses over the years. Similarly, the Unification Church has been monitored by law enforcement agencies and is considered both highly controlling and potentially, extremely dangerous. Both Christian and Jewish organizations have condemned the UC, despite its claims of Judeo-Christian themes.

94. For Allez Vous consultants, district managers, executive district managers, and executive area managers only.

95. Dana, D. (2020). *Polyvagal exercises for safety and connection: 50 client-centered practices*. Norton & Company.

96. Niles, B., et al. (2022). *Tai chi and qigong for trauma-exposed populations: A systematic review. Mental Health and Physical Activity, 22*. The authors point out the lack of large studies needed but hypothesize on the mechanisms of helping trauma symptoms. My opinion on the whole of the literature of various movement approaches is that they likely share the same brain-body mechanics in terms of vagal engagement, so they all probably offer comparable benefits for healing trauma and stress.

97. Little Ouchies. A Cleveland-based company makes these (go, North Coast!). I'm sure there are similar things on the market, and I suspect they offer similar benefits, but this is one I use with my clients. Plus, they come in bright colors with fun names—just saying!

98. Church, D., et al. (2018). *Guidelines for the treatment of PTSD using clinical EFT (Emotional Freedom Techniques). Healthcare*, 6(4), 146. This article specifically discusses addressing PTSD symptoms using EFT but references that hundreds of trials indicate the effectiveness of this approach. For sub-clinical (everyday) uses, check out EFT International for free materials, or of course seek out a professional who is trained in the more in-depth practices.

99. Cramer, T. (2017, February 21). *Can yoga ease your PTSD? VA wants to find out. Veterans Health Administration.*

100. Fans of Elizabeth Gilbert will recognize my adaptation of her narration of meditating in *Eat, Pray, Love*—but you may also recognize it from your own mind.

101. The ZdoggMD Show Podcast with Dr. Zubin Damania.

102. Khoudari, L. (2021). *Lifting heavy things: Healing trauma one rep at a time.* Lifetree.

103. Lamott, A. (2000). *Traveling mercies: Some thoughts on faith.* Anchor.

104. Maté, G. and Maté, D. (2022). *The myth of normal: Trauma, illness and healing in a toxic culture.* Avery.

105. Ibid.

106. Hesiod (n.d.). *Works and Days.*

107. They had this delicious hazelnut flavor, and I knew better than to ask what it was.

108. Lawrence, F. (Director). (2005). *Constantine* [Film]. Warner Bros.

109. American Psychiatric Association (2013). *The diagnostic and statistical manual of mental disorders* (5th ed.).

110. Maté, G. and Maté, D. (2022). *The myth of normal: Trauma, illness and healing in a toxic culture.* Avery.

111. Cozolino, L. (2024). *The neuroscience of psychotherapy: Healing the social brain* (4th ed.) W. W. Norton & Co.

112. Maté, G. and Maté, D. (2022). *The myth of normal: Trauma, illness*

and healing in a toxic culture. Avery.

113. Dahl, M. (2015, February). You're Not Losing Your Memory. You're Just Distracted. *New York Magazine.*

114. Stone, A. (2012). *Fooling Houdini: Magicians, mentalists, math geeks and the hidden powers of the mind.* Harper.

115. Ibid.

116. This is in no way meant to diminish people who choose these reminders. It's deeply personal, and our culture of lack is what I'm aiming at here, not the individual choices we make to combat it.

117. Noteberg, S. (2021). *Monotasking: How to focus your mind, be more productive, and improve your brain health.* Racehorse.

118. Branch, T. (2021). *Escaping the cybertrance* [Interview]. *Psychotherapy Networker Mindfulness Webcast.* https://www.psychotherapynetworker.org

119. Maté, G., & Maté, D. (2022). In *The myth of normal: Trauma, illness, and healing in a toxic culture.* p 29. Avery. They are quoting the great existential therapist Rollo May.

120. Hudson, H. (Director). (1981). *Chariots of Fire,* 20th Century-Fox. Yep, you guessed it, I had this one memorized from cable TV too. Ask me anything about British track and field in 1924.

121. Csikszentmihalyi, M. (1975). *Beyond boredom and anxiety: Experiencing flow in work and play.* Jossey-Bass, San Francisco. See also: (1990). *Flow: The psychology of optimal experience.* Harper and Row, New York.

122. Values in Action survey. University of Pennsylvania. https://ppc.sas.upenn.edu/resources/questionnaires-researchers/survey-character-strengths

123. Gonzalez, A., et al. (2018). Effect of exposure to similar flavours in sensory specific satiety: Implications for eating behaviour. *Appetite, 127,* [page range if known].

124. Maté, G., and Maté, D. (2022). *The Myth of normal: Trauma, illness and healing in a toxic culture.* Avery.

125. Berridge, K. & Kringelbach, M. (2015). Pleasure systems in the brain. *Neuron,* 86(3). Carter, C. (2014). Oxytocin pathways and the evolution of human behavior. *Annual Review of Psychology,* 65. Chaouloff, F., et al.

(1999). Serotonin and stress. *Neuropsychopharmacology,* 21(2). Duman, R., & Monteggia, L. (2006). A neurotrophic model for stress-related mood disorders. *Biological Psychiatry,* 59(12). Esch, T., & Stefano, G. (2004). The neurobiology of pleasure, reward processes, addiction and their health implications. *Neuroendocrinology Letters,* 25(4). Feder, A., et al. (2009). Psychobiology and molecular genetics of resilience. *Nature Reviews Neuroscience,* 10(6). Koepp, M., et al. (1998). Evidence for striatal dopamine release during a video game. *Nature, 393*(6682). Leknes, S., & Tracey, I. (2008). A common neurobiology for pain and pleasure. *Nature Reviews Neuroscience,* 9(4). Young, S. (2007). How to increase serotonin in the human brain without drugs. *Journal of Psychiatry & Neuroscience,* 32(6). Zak, P., et al. (2005). Oxytocin is associated with human trustworthiness. *Hormones and Behavior,* 48(5). Cited in Neurolaunch (2024). Happy Chemicals: Understanding Dopamine, Oxytocin, Serotonin, and Endorphins.

126. Gilbert, E. (2006). *Eat, pray, love: One woman's search for everything across Italy, India and Indonesia*. Penguin.

127. This popular quote of Muir's shows up in multiple versions and has been variously attributed, but the most reliable source I could find seems to be a note he wrote in a book of Ralph Waldo Emerson essays. http://oberlin.edu.physics/dyster/Muir/QuotableJohnMuir.

128. Except this book, obviously.

129. Hutton, R. (2019). *The triumph of the moon: A history of modern pagan witchcraft*. Oxford University Press.

130. Fred Rogers Institute. (n.d.). Saint Vincent College.

131. Redmond, L., & Mokhtarian, P. (2001). The positive utility of the commute: Modeling ideal commute time and relative desired commute amount. *Transportation,* 28(2), [179-205].

132. Larkin Hall, the old, comfortably shabby one, not the new RPAC, which looks like it could launch a very fit colony on Mars if need be.

133. I maintained this ritual most Friday afternoons for the first few years of my practice, until the tragic day when the OSU women's swim team started holding their practices at the same time, and my self-confidence knew when it was beaten.

134. McKnight, J. and Block, P. (2012). *The abundant community: Awakening the power of families and neighborhoods.* Berrett-Koehler Publishers.

135. Cortisol. My.Clevelandclinic.org.

136. Pun absolutely intended. I regret nothing!

137. Maté, G. and Maté, D. (2022). *The Myth of Normal: Trauma, Illness and Healing In a Toxic Culture.* Avery, New York.

138. Ibid.

139. Ibid.

140. Ibid.

141. Ibid.

142. Ibid.

143. Ibid.

144. Ibid.

145. Nakazawa, D. J. (2020). *The angel and the assassin: The tiny brain cell that changed the course of medicine.* Ballantine Books.

146. The correct medical plural name for these cells is *microglia*, but to make the reading easier, I'll refer to them as microglials, as they are also sometimes called.

147. Oligodendrocytes, astrocytes, and ependymals are the other three. If you've heard of any of these, it might be *astrocytes*, as in the brain tumors called *astrocytomas*.

148. Nakazawa, D. (2020). *The angel and the assassin: The tiny brain cell that changed the course of medicine.* Ballantine Books.

149. Ibid.

150. Ibid.

151. Ibid.

152. Miller, K., et al. (2017). Sleep and dreaming in posttraumatic stress disorder. *Current psychiatry reports, 19*(10), 71. See also van der Kolk, B. (2015). *The body keeps the score: Brain, mind and body in the healing of trauma.* Penguin Books.

153. Bolz-Weber, N. (2023, June 4). *1% less asshole.* The Corners. https://thecorners.substack.com/p/1-less-asshole

154. Lamott, A. (1999). *Traveling mercies: Some thoughts on faith.* Pantheon.

155. Ibid.

156. I checked the current medical literature, but as of this writing, Donkey Fever remains unknown outside of weird Italian morality fables. More research needed.

157. Lamott, A. (1999). *Traveling mercies: Some thoughts on faith.* Pantheon.

158. To learn more about Edi's work in leadership and well-being, you can go to her website: edipasalis.com.

159. Rabbi Tarfon, *Pirkei Avot,* 2:16.

160. Kalsched, D. (2013). *Trauma and the soul: A psycho-spiritual approach to human development and its interruption.* Routledge.

161. Bowler, K. (2019, TEDmed). "Everything happens for a reason"—and other lies I've loved. TEDmed. https://www.tedmed.com/talk/everything-happens-for-a-reason-and-other-lies-ive-loved/

162. Carpenter, M. Chapin. (1996). *Dead man walking (A dream like this).* On *Dead man walking: Music from and inspired by the motion picture.* Columbia Records.

ABOUT THE AUTHOR

Lara Palay, MSW, LISW-S is a psychotherapist with nearly 30 years in private practice specializing in trauma and loss. A co-founder of Aldridge Palay Consulting, Ms. Palay started her career as an hourly worker in the mental health field and went on to be a supervisor and clinical director for multiple mental health agencies. In addition to clinical practice, she has taught social work graduate students for more than a decade.

Ms. Palay served as the project manager for the Mental Illness and Developmental Disabilities Coordinating Center of Excellence for the state of Ohio, helping to advance trauma awareness in dual diagnosis. She is the author of *The Way Through: Trauma Responsive Care for Intellectual and Developmental Disability Professionals*.

Ms. Palay lives with her husband and a random assortment of spoiled pets.

9 798994 234501